How Do You Baptize a Whale?

How Do You Baptize a Whale?

An Encouragement to Compassion

ANDREW KADEL

Foreword by Rebecca Lyman

WIPF & STOCK · Eugene, Oregon

HOW DO YOU BAPTIZE A WHALE?
An Encouragement to Compassion

Copyright © 2025 Andrew Kadel. All rights reserved. Except for brief quotations in critical publications or reviews, no part of this book may be reproduced in any manner without prior written permission from the publisher. Write: Permissions, Wipf and Stock Publishers, 199 W. 8th Ave., Suite 3, Eugene, OR 97401.

Wipf & Stock
An Imprint of Wipf and Stock Publishers
199 W. 8th Ave., Suite 3
Eugene, OR 97401

www.wipfandstock.com

PAPERBACK ISBN: 979-8-3852-5620-4
HARDCOVER ISBN: 979-8-3852-5621-1
EBOOK ISBN: 979-8-3852-5622-8

10/06/25

Unless otherwise indicated, all scriptural quotations are from the New Revised Standard Version of the Bible, copyright ©1989 by the Division of Christian Education of the National Council of Churches of Christ in the U.S.A. and are used by permission.

Quotations from the Revised Standard Version of the Bible are copyright ©1946, 1952, and 1971 National Council of Churches of Christ in the United States of America and are used by permission.

This book is dedicated to the people of Trinity Episcopal Church of Morrisania, Bronx, New York, and in loving memory of Father Wendell Roberts, their rector from 1950 to 1992.

Contents

	Foreword by Rebecca Lyman	ix
	Preface	xiii
	Acknowledgments	xvii
	Abbreviations	xix
	Prologue	1
1	A Big Universe	5
2	*Homo Technicus*: The Tool User	12
	This Idaho: Funeral homily for Don Kadel	20
3	The World Where I Grew Up	22
	On Asparagus and Being a Neighbor	31
4	The Heart of the Text	34
5	A Wedding Feast	43
6	Jesus the Healer	52
7	Casting Out Demons	61
8	The Resurrection of Jesus	72
9	The Spirit and the Church	84
10	The Deep	93
	Te Deum Laudamus	102
	For Further Reading	105
	Bibliography	109

Foreword

IN THIS WONDERFUL EXPLORATION of compassion from the depths of the universe to his own many years in ministry throughout the United States, Drew Kadel offers us an encouragement to wonder, to repent, to understand, and to love as we inhabit God's vast and interconnected creation. In his first chapter, he explores our human self-consciousness within the recent scientific conceptions of the universe and our growing understanding of the other sentient beings around us. He then weaves together his own experience growing up as a descendent of settlers in the Western United States, with its natural beauty and hidden history of violence, to a precise examination of the life and work of Jesus as a healer and a teacher. He then turns to his own disappointments and transformations in his later ministry. The gifts of the experience of working with an African American parish in New York included a time of renewal and reality about the heart of the good news.

These are not all easy stories. These are not all familiar Bible readings. The author is deeply attuned to our deceptions inside white American culture and routine ecclesiastical politics, as well as in ourselves. Placing our own lived experiences of the world more precisely into the vastness of God as focused through the healing and compassionate life of Jesus, we may begin to discern the abundant life which surges around and through all faithful struggles for this world and one another. Compassion alone heals us and our suffering world through solidarity, respect, and acknowledgment: we are only a small part of the vast energy of grace which pervades and redeems all reality. How, in light of the wideness of God's mercy, do you baptize a whale?

Are American churches today places of healing and compassion? Do we follow or even allow the presence and power of divine compassion in the Holy Spirit, the advocate for those on the margins or left out of the

Foreword

white myths of prosperity? Divine compassion as practiced and lived in solidarity with others, including other beings in God's good creation, is the source of hope and life for us all. Widening our minds and hearts allows the necessary amendment of life for us to thrive together as compassionate followers of Jesus in the divine way of justice and mercy. This book gives us a needed challenge and comfort by offering the wisdom from a life of ministry and faithful searching.

> REBECCA LYMAN
> Garrett Professor of Church History Emerita
> The Church Divinity School of the Pacific

My *brother*, the Church is the family of God, the body of Christ, and the temple of the Holy Spirit. All baptized people are called to make Christ known as Savior and Lord, and to share in the renewing of his world. Now you are called to work as pastor, priest, and teacher, together with your bishop and fellow presbyters, and to take your share in the councils of the Church.

As a priest, it will be your task to proclaim by word and deed the Gospel of Jesus Christ, and to fashion your life in accordance with its precepts. You are to love and serve the people among whom you work, caring alike for young and old, strong and weak, rich and poor. You are to preach, to declare God's forgiveness to penitent sinners, to pronounce God's blessing, to share in the administration of Holy Baptism and in the celebration of the mysteries of Christ's Body and Blood, and to perform the other ministrations entrusted to you.

In all that you do, you are to nourish Christ's people from the riches of his grace, and strengthen them to glorify God in this life and in the life to come.

My *brother*, do you believe that you are truly called by God and his Church to this priesthood?

Examination from the Ordination of a Priest, 1979 ***Book of Common Prayer*, 531.**

Preface

I HAVE BEEN A priest for a very long time, by far the majority of my life. In the Christian church, the word "priest" is used interchangeably with the word "presbyter." That word presbyter means *old*. For a twenty-seven-year-old, that was a somewhat puzzling and, frankly, difficult burden to bear, but now that I've passed the mark of "three score and ten," it's just who I am.

At my ordination, as in the ordination of all priests in the Episcopal Church, the bishop read a text explaining the obligations of a presbyter, so I knew what I was signing on for. In short, together with the bishop and fellow presbyters, I was undertaking to: *proclaim by word and deed the Gospel of Jesus Christ; be a pastor, a priest, a teacher; and to take my share in the councils of the church*. Sometimes, I think certain church authorities would rather that I didn't understand that last part as an obligation to call problems with our church to their attention. But, again, that's who I am, and I have been living with that burden for a very long time.

This is a book written from the perspective of an old priest reflecting on and teaching what I've learned as a pastor, preacher, and participant in the world that includes the church. I spent a large part of my career as a theological librarian, so I'm acquainted with scholars and scholarship, but, though I sometimes resort to footnotes, this is not meant to be a scholarly kind of work. Rather, it's meant as an encouragement for people to live truly as we are meant to live: as compassionate and decent human beings, in a world that isn't just about us.

Humility has been a major interest of mine, especially as I came to appreciate the painful consequences of my own arrogance and grandiosity. As I've reflected on this, it became clear that arrogance characterizes much of humanity, which can lead to disastrous effects on fellow human beings and the world as a whole. I have come to believe that this arrogance isn't merely a fault in individuals, but characterizes humanity as a whole—a characteristic from which we can and must repent.

Understanding human arrogance and the path to humility is not a simple thing—most quick explanations of humility end up creating false impressions, often disempowering or exploiting people rather than helping them move forward to a more compassionate and joyful life. This is why this book is shaped as it is: starting out with situating us in the universe (actually, it's more a matter of inviting you into my universe and world, and illustrations often are from my own experience); then examining the most distinctive aspect of the human species: making and using tools; and then finishing with the historical world in which we find ourselves. Being grounded in who we are is important before approaching the theological questions that follow: the heart of the religion of Israel, Jesus' place and ministry in Galilee, his life as a healer and exorciser of demons, and his Resurrection. Then I seek to understand the Holy Spirit, the Spirit of compassion, through an appreciation and critique of the church through my own experience of it. The conclusion returns to our place in the universe, but this time in the Deep, the beginning of Creation, in which we have our beginning and end, but now in equality and communion with all of God's creatures.

This book is not about the church; it's not about ways to win; it's not even particularly humanistic—if we understand that term to mean that humans are the most important of all things in this universe. We are a particular sort of creature and we could be content with that. But, inclined as we are to measure everything by ourselves, we describe "man as the measure of all things."[1]

I hope that some who are not Christians will read this book, since it's not particularly "churchy," or encouraging people to be that way. It is, nonetheless, from a Christian priest's perspective, exploring the positive values that underlie the message of Jesus as a way to talk about our small place in the vastness of the universe; or, according to Heb 11:3, "By faith we understand that the worlds were prepared by the word of God, so that what is seen was made from things that are not visible."

But always, Jesus is my particular focus. He is the embodiment of what is true in our religion and in our wider culture, as non-religious as it

---

1. A quote attributed to the pre-Socratic philosopher Protagoras, often cited by Renaissance and, later, Enlightenment philosophers. I insert the patriarchal use of generic "man" here to emphasize the arrogance of humanity in thinking this. Patriarchy is only a major aspect of the generalized arrogance of humanity.

Preface

purports to be. It's not a matter of finding out what he taught, but the way in which he confronted the spiritual forces of his age—a time that was very fraught, not unlike our own. When the full picture comes into focus, it is clear—there is one thing that is true, one thing that Jesus embodies, and one thing that is the origin of all things. And that one thing is compassion.

This book was written before the 2024 election. Under current circumstances, it is even more important for everyone to be encouraged to a life of compassion, and the courage to face those who scoff at compassion, selfishly terrorizing those most in need of it.

Acknowledgments

FIRST AND FOREMOST, I must acknowledge the contributions of my beloved wife, Paula Schaap. Besides her support and love for me through many times, both joyous and difficult, Paula worked with me on this book from its inception. She critiqued my ideas and made suggestions of what should be included or left out. I included "On Asparagus and Being a Neighbor" on her suggestion and that helped to shape the entire book. She is a professional editor, and she edited two entire drafts of this book before submission. This book would not have been completed without her work.

I also want to thank my colleagues and friends, Deirdre Good and Atkinson Davenport. Both of them examined early drafts and made suggestions for improvements, especially in the biblical exegesis sections. Special thanks to David Hurd who provided the images for the musical notation for the *Te Deum Laudamus*.

In a reflective personal book, such as this one, the people who helped to form the author are primary and essential sources. I have dedicated this book to Trinity Episcopal Church in the south Bronx, and I discuss my debt to them in chapter nine. St. James Episcopal Church in Lincoln, California, and Calvary Episcopal Church in Flemington, New Jersey, are two congregations where I benefited from serving as their interim pastor. I appreciate their love and compassion and their hard work in reshaping themselves in their search for permanent pastoral leadership. Their leaders and members continue to be my friends. Rob Voyle helped me to learn how to be an effective interim pastor to these congregations in his course on "Appreciative Inquiry."

Heartfelt thanks to Professor Rebecca Lyman for her generous foreword, which accurately casts this book in its most positive light.

Thank you to my colleagues and students at General Theological Seminary, Wesley Theological Seminary, and Union Theological Seminary. Your

Acknowledgments

insight and support helped encourage me to grow, especially as a pastor and theologian. I especially want to acknowledge two colleagues of blessed memory from Union Theological Seminary: Seth Kasten, my supervisor and then co-worker, who helped me to become a member of the American Theological Library Association, and Milton McCormick Gatch, director of the Burke Library and a continuing mentor. I send my particular love and gratitude to Mary Robison, the reference librarian at General Theological Seminary; to Deirdre Good, David Hurd, Pat Malloy, Amy Lamborn, Joshua Davis, Andrew Irving, and the late Mitties DeChamplain, the members of our faculty union; and to Hershey Mallette Stephens, whose graduation sermon perfectly summed up a time when the love and compassion of a community was essential in bringing us through safely and whole at the end.

Abbreviations

OLD TESTAMENT

Gen	Genesis
Exod	Exodus
Lev	Leviticus
Num	Numbers
Deut	Deuteronomy
Josh	Joshua
Judg	Judges
Ruth	Ruth
1–2 Sam	1–2 Samuel
1–2 Kgs	1–2 Kings
1–2 Chr	1–2 Chronicles
Ezra	Ezra
Neh	Nehemiah
Esth	Esther
Job	Job
Ps/Pss	Psalm/Psalms
Prov	Proverbs
Eccl	Ecclesiastes
Song	Song of Songs
Isa	Isaiah
Jer	Jeremiah
Lam	Lamentations
Ezek	Ezekiel
Dan	Daniel
Hos	Hosea

ABBREVIATIONS

Joel	Joel
Amos	Amos
Obad	Obadiah
Jonah	Jonah
Mic	Micah
Nah	Nahum
Hab	Habakkuk
Zeph	Zephaniah
Hag	Haggai
Zech	Zechariah
Mal	Malachi

NEW TESTAMENT

Matt	Matthew
Mark	Mark
Luke	Luke
John	John
Acts	Acts
Rom	Romans
1–2 Cor	Corinthians
Gal	Galatians
Eph	Ephesians
Phil	Philippians
Col	Colossians
1–2 Thess	1–2 Thessalonians
1–2 Tim	1–2 Timothy
Titus	Titus
Phlm	Philemon
Heb	Hebrews
Jas	James
1–2 Pet	1–2 Peter
1–2–3 John	1–2–3 John
Jude	Jude
Rev	Revelation

Prologue

I bind unto myself today
the virtues of the star-lit heaven
the glorious sun's life-giving ray,
the whiteness of the moon at even,
the flashing of the lightning free,
the whirling wind's tempestuous shocks,
the stable earth, the deep salt sea,
around the old eternal rocks.
—Hymn attributed to St. Patrick

In May of 2014, Pope Francis preached a homily in which he criticized a group of priests who were refusing to baptize the children of women whose style of life they disapproved. The thing that got the attention of the world press, however, was an offhand comment he made during the homily: "I would baptize anyone who came to me. I would even baptize a Martian if he asked."[1] That comment got me thinking: What could it even mean to baptize a Martian? The pope was making an offhand illustration; it isn't a considered theological policy. But most people understood what he meant, and many share the sentiment. What we know about Mars makes it pretty clear that it doesn't currently host complex, intelligent life of the sort that the term "Martian" evokes. However, many hope that complex intelligent life will be discovered somewhere in the galaxy, so Francis is using an old

1. AFP, "Pope Says Baptism."

term for "space alien." That seemed strange to me—Christian baptism is always reserved for people because it is literally immersion in the story of Jesus: living as a human being, being executed by human beings, dying on a cross, then being raised from the dead. I was surprised that many of my clergy colleagues appeared to agree with Pope Francis: if an alien was properly sentient, with moral sensibility and understanding, then they could be baptized and partake of the salvation offered by Christ, provided they chose that path. Granted, like me and other members of the generation that grew up in the 1960s and 1970s, these colleagues tend to be fans of *Star Trek* and *Star Wars*. Who wouldn't offer baptism to Worf or Chewbacca, after all?[2] But these creatures are consistently depicted as humanoid and, as storylines go along, their sensibilities become increasingly human. We anthropomorphize nonhuman life to the point that they are no longer truly alien. Personally, I am most charmed by the *Star Wars* character R2D2, the droid who looks like a public trash receptacle. (Who knows what immersion in water would do to a droid's circuitry?)

So that was the impetus that led me to write this book.

Over the past couple of decades, I've lived at very close quarters with dogs, and it's clear to me that they think, understand, anticipate, and have emotions in ways that aren't so dissimilar from humans.[3] No one seriously argues we should baptize dogs. Many reasons are put forward, such as that dogs don't have enough intelligence or self-consciousness, or something like that—but really, it's that dogs and other intelligent, nonhuman creatures live in ways that are incommensurate with human ways of living.

Then there are creatures that share our planet with us that scientists posit have intelligence and self-awareness, perhaps even beyond that of humans. They might not have our propensity for toolmaking, which may be a consequence of our opposable thumbs, but they surpass us in many ways. Our domestic cats and dogs have a keener sense of smell and hearing. And then, there's the matter of our much vaunted brains that we believe is the reason we can exercise dominion over the earth. Except the brains of whales and elephants are larger than ours. But, more importantly, those

---

2. The Christian foreign missionary movement of the nineteenth and twentieth centuries is often viewed as an adjunct to colonialism and European and American exploitation of people around the world, which is simply a fact. There were, however, some foreign missionaries who truly served and cared for the people they lived among and I regard my colleagues who want to baptize space aliens as the successors to that sort of missionary.

3. Of course, I can't prove that humans think or have emotions, but I believe they do.

animals demonstrate very complex social structures. Elephants have been observed remembering individuals that they haven't seen for many years and whales have complex communication systems, which might be regarded as analogous to what humans call language; perhaps those communication systems are even more sophisticated than human language. Both elephants and whales clearly demonstrate grief when their companions or their young die, especially when they are killed by human beings.

As I was thinking about how things do not fit neatly into the hierarchies humans have drawn up, a small hawk, perhaps a kite, flew over our terrace in our high-rise apartment building. Though "birdbrained" is a human derogatory expression implying stupidity, we know that many birds, such as crows and parrots, are very intelligent. We know this about parrots in part because those in captivity can speak human languages. This doesn't mean that the hawk that flew by, which avoids close contact with humans, isn't even smarter—its decision to keep away from us might be proof of that.

We have a very large universe with many creatures nothing like ourselves but equal in dignity and holiness to human beings. Pope Francis made a good-natured, joking offer to baptize a Martian. Yet, what should we say about baptizing a whale or other creatures in our universe that are at least as alien?

1

A Big Universe

Space is big. You just won't believe how vastly, hugely, mind-bogglingly big it is. I mean, you may think it's long way down the road to the chemist's, but that's just peanuts to space.

—Douglas Adams, *A Hitchhiker's Guide to the Galaxy*

THE UNIVERSE IS REALLY big.

And by really big, what I mean is inconceivably big. No one can hold in their minds how large it is. We use surrogates in place of comprehension, but even our most capacious minds can't comprehend the depth of the distance between the galaxies. We just build ciphers upon estimates upon guesses because those approximations are satisfactory for what are currently our very finite purposes. Perhaps that's what we always do with our imaginations, but the universe is not built on a human scale and humans are not built on a universal scale.[1]

---

1. That's something I've always enjoyed about Terry Pratchett and Neil Gaiman's *Good Omens*: their satirical universe dates only to 4004 BCE, which is the date Archbishop Ussher calculated in the seventeenth century by tracing back and adding together the sequence of all the events in the Bible. Heaven and hell are populated by a bureaucracy of demons (and angels, but those angels are every bit as demonic as the demons) and the universe is on a human scale, ultimately coming down to a small boy, his dog, and some friends in a small English village. I'm afraid that the universe is bigger and more complicated, perhaps as scary, but I hope not nearly so petty in its ultimate structure or ends.

How Do You Baptize a Whale?

One estimate is that there are two hundred sextillion stars in the universe. That is to say, there are about one hundred billion stars in our own galaxy, the Milky Way, and there are probably about two trillion galaxies in the detectable universe. And that assumes, as far as present-day knowledge takes us, the Milky Way is an unremarkable, middling galaxy and that the sample of the far, ultra deep space sky that the Hubble Space Telescope took of very distant galaxies is typical of the rest of space. Thus, that number of galaxies times the estimated number of stars in our average galaxy yields two hundred sextillion.

Let's try that in numeral form:

Two hundred sextillion works out to:	200,000,000,000,000,000,000,000
Two trillion would be:	2,000,000,000,000
The more down-to-earth one hundred billion is:	100,000,000,000

A few years ago, I made a rough calculation of how far a photon would have traveled since the big bang: 80 sextillion, 268 quintillion, 300 quadrillion miles.

Again, in numerals:	80,268,300,000,000,000,000,000

And before any scientist or statistician reading this points out that my rough guesstimate isn't accurate to that many significant digits, let's cut the difference and say:

$$80{,}000{,}000{,}000{,}000{,}000{,}000{,}000$$

Which is probably as accurate and more elegantly written because when you're dealing with the unfathomable, 268 quintillion miles and change loses its significance.

Of course, when I go back to Google and calculate again, I come up with a different answer: 81,130,230,000,000,000,000,000. This is what happens when people who mostly studied theology try to horn in on scientists. We're stuck falling back on the internet, which I assure you is a risky business, at best.

In any case, that's a lot of zeros. Scientists think so, too, so they came up with scientific notation, which knocks off the zeros and replaces them with exponents:

A Big Universe

2 trillion	=	2×10^{12}
100 million	=	10^8
200 sextillion	=	2×10^{23}
80 sextillion 268 quadrillion	=	80.268×10^{21}

And so on. The notation makes the numbers more compact, easier to manipulate, and do complicated calculations with. But ultimately, it's just a lot of incomprehensible zeros adding up to very big—incomprehensibly big—and not much more.[2]

Scientists measure, infer, and estimate, and it yields useful results, but the distance itself? More dark, more cold, more heat, or more light than anyone could tolerate or imagine experiencing. In the space between galaxies, there are places where the naked eye would not be able to even detect any light—too far to even see the glimmer of distant galaxies without a telescope.

The summer after I graduated from high school in Caldwell, Idaho, I worked for a man who salvaged steel from oil fields. The newly founded Environmental Protection Agency was pressuring oil companies to clean up the mess they were making of God's good earth. So, the oil companies contracted with a lot of unscrupulous guys like my boss who never met a corner he couldn't cut, including taking advantage of kids by paying a weekly salary that, if we had worked forty hours, would have been the minimum wage (which in 1968 was $1.65 an hour). Except our days sometimes went from dawn to well past sunset. It was exhausting work, lifting and cutting heavy steel in the southern Idaho summer sun.

One day, I was told to bring a suitcase with a few weeks' clothing. When I arrived at the worksite, we got into the cab of an eighteen-wheeler and set off for central Wyoming, where the boss had picked up a job collecting steel rods. I remember listening on the truck's radio to the roll call at the Democratic National Convention where George McGovern was nominated as we drove through the arid grasslands in western Wyoming.

We made a pit stop at a hilltop at about 2:00 a.m., miles from even a farmhouse, let alone a town. I stepped out on the shoulder, looked up, and realized that the sky was filled with more stars than even I, a kid from the country, had ever imagined. It wasn't only that the Milky Way was visible,

---

2. The distance across the universe is actually much further than how far a photon would have traveled since the big bang. Rather than 13.8 billion light-years, the estimated distance across the observable universe is about ninety-three billion light-years, due to the universe expanding in all directions during that time.

it was that the stars I knew were brighter than I had ever seen them before, and the spaces between them were filled in with so many, many stars. The sky seemed huger than before and almost white with stars. It may have been the first time I had an inkling of what the psalmist meant when he wrote, "The whole earth is filled with awe at your wonders; where morning dawns, where evening fades, you call forth songs of joy" (Ps 65:8).

Human beings imagine many things. It could well be argued that imagination is the essential characteristic of being human. I'm not sure that's right, though I do believe that one thing we humans imagine is that we understand things how they "really are"—that we can comprehend this world and use that comprehension to control it, projecting that control out into infinity. The one thing about our lives that truly knows no bounds is human arrogance.

So, when we're considering the width, the length, and the height[3] of the scope of the universe, what we should understand is that human beings are continuously tempted to believe that they think like God—that they comprehend the nature of things, that their observations of regularities in the systems we live in show that us humans partake in ultimate wisdom. And our scientists, being human, aren't immune from that way of thinking.

I have no beef with science. I delight in what science has achieved and look forward to ways that it will expand our knowledge and improve life on earth. In fact, as I understand it as a lay person, the scientific method, properly understood and implemented, is a humble affair. Things are observed. They are measured and written down. Then the scientist looks at those things, wonders how they might fit with other things, and makes a prediction—really, a guess. Then comes a plan to test that prediction. Experiments are designed and records are made of what happens when experiments are carried out. If the predictions have accurately predicted the outcomes, then the data in these records will reflect that. If enough trials result in outcomes consistent with a prediction, then that original guess is treated as knowledge of something that is true. If information comes back that is not consistent with the original guess, then it needs to be modified. In good science, hypotheses are modified all the time in response to new information. In principle, science is self-correcting, since all errors are acknowledged and any guess, hypothesis, theory, or theorem will be readjusted or even abandoned as necessary. But scientists are people and, therefore, subject to the same shortcomings as anyone else.

---

3. To somewhat misapply the words of Eph 3:18.

People can be selfless, generous, and humble. But most of us are that way only some of the time. There are also those times when we're anxious, defensive, and petty—doing things and saying things that will protect our standing with others or help us get ahead, even just a little bit. This isn't even counting those who are forthrightly dishonest and evil—those people exist, but I don't need to mention them in making the point that I want to make here. Even people who are very intelligent and well-educated, who have fundamentally good intentions, don't always see and express things clearly and honestly. Distortions result from fear of failure or loss of status. Arguments are made from weak results; choices are made to eliminate "outliers" from averages.

Ultimately, research will catch up to errors and distortions. Enough results will eventually correct misestimates or change false directions from misinterpretation of data. But it takes much longer than most believe—often years or even decades—especially in areas of inquiry where few studies are done or where data from any experiment is sparse. "Publish or perish" is an ever-present reality in every academic and scientific field, and most of the people involved choose not to perish. Sometimes that involves shaving the edges of the truth, or neglecting to point out problems with our data.

None of this refutes the scientific method. Nor does it imply any moral problem with scientists in general. At least, not any problem that is not shared across-the-board by all human beings. But it's all too common to see or hear someone say "I believe science," and what they're talking about is what they think are hard and fast results—not referring to an iterative method where results are always being adjusted—but hard and fast results that are magically true because they are reported by scientists.

All results are, to some degree, approximate. All theories are subject to change. Laws of nature are observed regularities that continue to be observed and then adjusted. We are sometimes fooled because particularly careful thinkers, like Sir Isaac Newton, make a lot of effort, incorporating a lot of observations, to formulate descriptions that work for predicting what will happen in all the circumstances we usually encounter. It is tempting, therefore, to say that Newton's law of gravitation is a description of the nature of the universe, rather than a description of observed regularities. The problem is, of course, Albert Einstein. Or rather, all the things that were happening in physics around the early twentieth century, which began to generate questions that Newton's laws couldn't explain. It's common enough to hear people try to explain this away by saying Newton was wrong, and now Einstein has described the nature of the universe as it is. But that isn't what happened.

How Do You Baptize a Whale?

Einstein and other modern-day physicists examined details that Newton never had an opportunity to examine. Without Newton's work, it's doubtful that later scientists would have had the tools to look at questions, both bigger and smaller, than his seventeenth or eighteenth-century contemporaries would have even begun to examine. Gravity, atoms, matter, energy, light—all have aspects of their behavior in certain circumstances that are not consistent with Newton's laws. Relativity and quantum theory describe regularities that we don't notice in our everyday lives. It takes a lot of work in mathematics and physics to make them align with common sense.[4]

Yet even as modern physics, whether theoretical or applied, continues to develop, there is no reason to think that anyone working in those fields is describing the underlying nature of the universe as it is. All scientists, including the most sophisticated quantum cosmologists, are noting and recording observed regularities and anomalies. Their theories are important because they are useful in one way or another. At some point in a few hundred or a few thousand years, those theories will be superseded. The best of them will be regarded as accurate for their time and available testing methods, like Newton or Aristotle before them.

"There are more things in heaven and earth, Horatio | Than are dreamt of in your philosophy."[5] Hamlet's not slighting his fellow student's beliefs or mental acuity. Rather, the Danish prince is questioning philosophy's—in Shakespeare's day, what we now call science was "natural philosophy"—restriction of all interpretations to the observable world.

Real life is hard. At best, everyone has disappointments and failures. Eventually, we all lose someone or something very important to us and we grieve. Even in the midst of triumph, there is loss. The temptation is to see everything in terms of how it affects us—how it affects me as an individual, in terms of my immediate wants, or how it affects the goals of my community or our country. Sometimes we think in bigger terms and frame our values as for the good of all humanity, perhaps even future humanity. Of course, we are nothing if we aren't human, so we do have to prioritize humanity.

---

4. Some philosophers scoff at "common sense" as insufferably naïve, even dangerous. But to me, common sense is the shared ability to grasp facts and concepts that work their way into a culture. Those who are naïve understand common sense concepts to be self-evident and irrefutable, but it is more that they have become integrated into the rest of shared knowledge that the vast majority of people understand. Ultimately, the basics of clear concepts work their way into common sense, though they might have originally been esoteric or counterintuitive.

5. Shakespeare, *Yale Shakespeare*, 987.

A Big Universe

But understanding human wants and struggles is not the same thing as understanding the universe, or even our own earth. Our context is within all the systems of this world that make that world possible. And most of that is not human. Not only that, it is a big problem to reduce the significance of the living and nonliving systems of our world to how they support human life and how they can be manipulated by humans to support their own existence. We aren't that wise. Reducing the world to objects to be manipulated has had devastating effects on our world—short-run gains that result in famines, deserts, slavery, and wars. There are wonderful things we know about that give life and beauty to our world that have no relationship to human effort or benefit, and there are many more mysteries to be discovered. This applies to living things, but also to those things we don't call living—often complex systems of incredible beauty—that we don't understand and perhaps, in principle, can never understand. The universe is a very big place after all.

To return to that summer job I had when I was a teenager for a moment: After a long day in Gillette, Wyoming, loading sucker rods onto that truck, another young guy and I were sent to spend two weeks at an oil field near Newcastle on Wyoming's eastern edge. We cut and banded together pipes and other useful steel to be loaded on that same truck that was scheduled to show back up on a Tuesday. Tuesday came and the truck mysteriously didn't show. Apparently, the driver, who in other parts of his life rode bulls in rodeos, had hooked up with a lady in Jackson Hole and didn't think spending an extra couple of days there mattered. I had to be back in Boise, Idaho, by Sunday so I could meet people to drive up to choir camp in Ghost Ranch, New Mexico—the same Ghost Ranch where Georgia O'Keefe painted some of her best-known landscapes—so we got ready to leave Friday. As we were finishing dinner at a Newcastle diner, the truck drove up. The driver and my partner took off to go back and load up the truck, and I took the boss's pickup truck for the thousand-mile drive back to Boise by myself.

I tried to power through that night on bad gas station coffee and junk food, driving through the Wind River Reservation in the blackness, with wisps of mist intermittently obstructing my view. Finally, I was too exhausted, so I pulled off and slept for a while. It was about 4:30 or 5:00 in the morning—pre-dawn—when I reached a place where the forest I had been driving through opened up over a wide valley and I could see Jackson Lake with low clouds above it. Above the lake, I could see the Grand Teton looming up with clouds encircling the bottom of the mountain. Tolkien's Middle-earth was nowhere near as magical.

2

Homo Technicus: The Tool User

> But who indeed are you, a human, to argue with God? Will what is molded say to the one who molds it, "Why have you made me like this?" Has the potter no right over the clay, to make out of the same lump one object for special use and another for ordinary use?
> —Romans 9:20–22

HUMAN BEINGS MAKE THINGS. Especially, we make tools. The thing that distinguishes humans from other animals the most is not language, and certainly not wisdom, but our universal practice of making and using tools. If someone had asked for my input on naming our species, I would have suggested *homo technicus*,[1] not *homo sapiens*. Technicus means a technician, someone who uses tools to solve problems and achieve goals, whether as an engineer, a craftsman, or even a scribe. *Sapiens* means wise, and I'm skeptical whether that really characterizes humanity. I spent the bulk of my working life as a librarian, primarily in theology libraries. A storehouse of wisdom! A place for reflection and discovery of deep truths!

---

1. Better Latin might be *homo faber*, as used by some Renaissance philosophers and, more recently, by Henri Bergson and Hannah Arendt. Their use of this term largely regards humans as makers and creators of something new, and thus, of a different, higher nature than animals. My use of this term is broader and less exalted than theirs. Humans are animals whose distinguishing characteristic is making and using tools. Other species have their own distinguishing characteristics.

Homo Technicus: The Tool User

In its own way, I suppose. But, in another way, all books are just tools in which to store words, and libraries are systems of tools to keep track of and take care of them.

One of the libraries where I served as director was at the General Theological Seminary in New York City. It was developed by Dean Eugene Hoffman in the nineteenth century. "The wealthiest clergyman in America!"—a newspaper proclaimed at the time.[2] Especially at that time, wealthy people were often collectors of art, stamps, and coins. Dean Hoffman collected books, and the seminary library gave him a rationale for collecting even more volumes than he would have for his private enjoyment. It was a showcase—the copy of the Gutenberg Bible Hoffman purchased put the library on the map.[3]

Among the seminary's library collections were Sumerian tablets. At one time, General Seminary had the oldest item listed on OCLC, the bibliographic database utility, which was a tablet more than three thousand years old. The Sumerian empire had the first libraries that I'm aware of. Priests in their huge temple complex engraved records on clay tablets, which were then baked to permanently preserve the information. These were then filed for future consultation. The bulk of these tablets were records of transactions for the operation of the economy of the empire. This economy was centered in the temple, so it made sense that priests were recording debits and credits. The economy did not use money, or at least there was no such thing as cash, so complex records kept things going. There were other texts as well. I'm not at all sure that the Sumerian priests recognized any difference between their recording of debits and credits and recording mythological narratives or ritual observances. It was an integrated whole—our modern notion that religion developed distinct from the conduct of empire or the economy isn't what actually happened.

These tablets were tools. Tools made with tools—tools used to mix the clay of the right consistency, styluses to make the strokes in cuneiform

---

2. I don't know exactly how much money he had, but in 1895 he sent a personal check for $15,000 to an English bookseller to purchase a Gutenberg Bible. As I'm writing this, an online inflation calculator says that's equivalent to about $500,000. See "Death of Dean Hoffman."

3. Quite literally. Decades after the Seminary had sold its copy of the Gutenberg Bible, I was sitting outside on the campus one weekend, enjoying the shade of the elm trees, when a Japanese tourist approached me and asked to see the Gutenberg Bible. When I explained to her that it was no longer there, she proffered her guidebook, which had a map of Manhattan showing General Theological Seminary, and she pointed to where it plainly said "Gutenberg Bible" in the text.

writing, and kilns to bake the clay. The tablets were tools that preserved information, locked it in objectively, outside of the uncertainty of human memory. The filing of them made it possible to retrieve the records so that people could exercise their credit or resolve disputes.

Books and libraries may be high order tools, serving abstraction and learning, but they are as much tools as knives or hammers or pots. Reading is using these tools, and language itself is built and refined along with the rest of our toolmaking.[4] When tools shift, language shifts. Indeed, major changes in communications technology, such as the development of the printing press, are accompanied by shifts, not only in language and expression, but in spirituality and religious observance.[5] Whenever I see someone define how humans are different from other animals, to the extent that it's credible, it comes down to language or toolmaking.

Often people use the word "technology" or "tech" and mean computers and the internet, along with other electronic gadgets and digital wizardry, distinguishing them from all previous technologies that relied on physical processes—big factories and machines with cogs, levers, and flywheels. One can make categories like that and also separate industrial machines from hand tools, for instance. But all of these are tools invented by people who worked from a basis of inherited technology and used their imagination to design something new to address a new situation or make it easier to do an existing job. Some inventions are true innovations, but many are simply applications of formulas invented by others to refine existing tools. For instance, the advantages of miniaturization of electronics arguably started with the invention of transistors in the 1950s. More miniaturization of ever more powerful units continues to this day, but this technology that we take for granted started with that shift to transistors. The amazing digital world is amazing because it does so many things so quickly, and new "generations" of these technologies occur close together. But these are still human tools doing human work, just replicating it faster than it has been done before.

---

4. Language, the communication between people with sounds, is not necessarily itself a tool. But the molding and standardizing of our language to fit what is written down in books or other media, or embedded in cultural practices, is clearly technological.

5. It's likely that we underestimate the ways in which technology (not just the internet but also things like radio and television) affect our social, religious, and spiritual cohesion and concepts. Anyone who thinks social media is intense in the way it allows one group to vilify another should read a few tracts from the sixteenth-century Reformation—quickly printed tracts made from a single printed sheet folded into a pamphlet and circulated widely. They were far harsher than Twitter.

Homo Technicus: The Tool User

Still, there is far more to the universe than human beings, human tools, and human language. We aspire to more: to know nature, to find other worlds, even to know the sources of the universe, the source of the material world, the source of life, the source of compassion—we aspire to know God. Yet anything that we describe or imagine is mediated through our limited, essentially crude tools of language, imaging, and recording observations. All is indirect and all is limited. Our images, imagination, and theories are, at best, fragmentary.

The third chapter of Genesis tells the story of the crafty serpent persuading the first naïve humans to eat the fruit of the tree of the knowledge of good and evil—the one fruit that had been forbidden them.[6] "But the serpent said to the woman, 'You will not die; for God knows that when you eat of it your eyes will be opened, and you will be like gods, knowing good and evil'" (Gen 3:4–5). The tempter asserts and the humans readily accept that this action of eating the fruit, and thus assimilating this knowledge, will make them gods, or at least godlike. Human imagination is like that—all too ready to believe that our imagination, thought, and language propel us into the realm of the infinite and the divine. Buzz Lightyear's slogan sums us up well: "To infinity and beyond!"[7]

I'm an optimist and, as an optimist, one of the things I enjoy is science fiction, especially the ways it tries to expand upon our better natures. Like *Star Trek*, which I remember as such a treat when I saw it as a kid when it was first broadcast on network TV. Even as a kid, I got that it was all about American ideals, projected forward into an imaginary future, and that it wasn't much different than the Westerns I also enjoyed (which took place not far from where I grew up). That childish enjoyment of the American ideal has given way to a more mature understanding of the way it has been used to oppress and deny many their humanity. At least the Klingons weren't human, so they were the bad guys and we could hate them without guilt. But then, of course, in later versions of *Star Trek*, the Klingons progressed

---

6. I highly recommend Wil Gafney's exegesis of this passage in *Womanist Midrash*, 20–25. Though I'm not qualified to unpack the subtleties of the Hebrew text, it's pretty clear that the interpretations of this passage in popular culture and received conventional Christian religion miss the mark in many significant ways. In particular, it's a mistake to elide the creation narrative of Gen 1:1—2:3 with the story in Gen 2:4—3:24. Genesis 1:26-28 and chapters 2–3 are two quite distinct ways of imagining humanity in the created universe. It's better to appreciate each separately before, or instead of, trying to combine or integrate them into a single worldview.

7. Lasseter, *Toy Story*.

to being allies with Lieutenant Worf as a sympathetic main character. Life's complicated.

Speculating, reflecting, and enjoying possibilities are good things. But it's also important to recognize how we are indulging ourselves, like I enjoy indulging in science fiction. Stories that focus on human activity triumphantly comprehending all the possibilities of the universe, going everywhere and doing everything with little apparent effort or complication, obscure the real beauty and depths of life and the universe.

Everything in this vast universe is comprised of systems of interacting variables: forces, matter, living creatures, thoughts, and feelings. These systems overlap and are layered over one another in myriad ways. Systems interacting with systems—systems of systems affecting one another in ways that we may or may not have some idea of what will result. We ourselves are complex systems, and so are our societies and beliefs. Without systems, life is inconceivable—but the friction and conflict within and between all the various systems make things harder as well.[8] Simple rational analysis of the implications of one set of factors won't reliably lead to accurate predictions or conclusions. Complex interactions of complex systems yield a world where no conclusion is ever final.

Systems are a way that our contemporaries seek to account for the complexity of reality as we experience it. It's as good a description as any, and more helpful than most in today's world. But like other scientific or theoretical descriptions, systems theory isn't describing reality as it is, but rather giving us a model to aid understanding. Another human tool for human purposes.

---

8. There are often distinct disciplines in divergent areas of study: physical sciences, biological sciences, social sciences, and various fields, where systems theory has been applied. One area that I'm acquainted with because of my training as an Episcopal priest is family systems theory that underlies some approaches to marriage and family counseling. It's often discovered during family counseling that, where one person is acting out because of mental illness, addiction, or some other behavioral problem, and that person (who has been identified as the "problem" in the family) starts to address their problems and change, other people in the family start displaying problematic behaviors. The family members seldom realize this is happening and often don't accept the connection when it's pointed out. Some family members may have built their identity around being the person that is helping their relative who has been identified as the problem. Others blame all the family's difficulties on that person, and when that begins to be resolved but difficulties in the system remain, they don't know who to blame. Sometimes, during the process of recovery, the identified patient gets clarity about abusive and exploitive things that have been happening to them and they start to resist. The important thing in this dynamic, as in all system dynamics, is that multiple factors are going on simultaneously, interacting and producing results that would not occur if there was only a single, well-understood cause.

Homo Technicus: The Tool User

We overestimate the significance of all of our tools. They are certainly important for our proximate purposes. If you don't have a hammer, you can't drive a nail, and if you don't drive the nail into the wall, how can you hang your picture?[9] But we want our tools to open the way to the big questions of the universe. Maybe if our language was good enough, and our use of it precise enough, we could get everything right—history and theology would end because we would have the final answers. This appears to be the ultimate goal of the current craze for artificial intelligence. Generative AI, like ChatGPT, is a way station on the way to artificial general intelligence (AGI), where machines will achieve consciousness and eventually incorporate all of human wisdom with all the advantages of computer technology as an autonomous solution to all of our problems. If this is a caricature, it's easy to find people aspiring to live as such caricatures. This is delusion, and a general misunderstanding of what this technology actually does. Machine learning has done lots of important things using complex iterative technology to help solve problems too big to address without it. It's a human invention, taking advantage of analogies of human methods of problem solving and enabling very fast machines to do the problem solving from many angles at once. These are amazing tools! But they don't show us the mind of God or solve the mystery of life.

It's odd that so many people look down on earlier cultures because they didn't have the same tools as we do. As if somehow smartphones make us smarter, or that flush toilets mean that we are concerned with cleanliness and our ancestors weren't. Tools are developed to solve identified problems—to improve the situation their inventors find themselves in. Mostly these are pretty desirable, at least the ones that are widely adopted and last for more than a few years. But it's a mistake to think that people in other circumstances did not have good lives, or reasonably so, or that our current tools have made everyone's life infinitely better in our day. Modern medicine has vastly reduced childhood mortality, and that's an unalloyed good. Yet everyone does die; we all suffer loss. The past few years in our culture and politics make it clear that people suffer oppression and violence, and people are as full of anxiety and fear as at any time in history despite more advanced tools than any previous generation has ever imagined. Often, new tools are invented just to ameliorate the bad effects of other tools. The internet was invented to bring people together and allow fast, widespread

---

9. I realize there are many advances in picture-hanging technology that don't involve nails, but all are technology and tools of some sort.

communication. But many recent inventions have been implemented to exploit access to people's personal information or to use social media to manipulate people in ways they'd never expected. And then resources are expended just to counter these adverse effects.[10]

Humans make tools to solve proximate problems, and usually those tools generate new proximate problems. Tools, of themselves, do not make us happier or more compassionate. In other words, they don't solve our most important human problems. This in and of itself would not be problematic. We solve the new problems; sometimes we investigate whether there might be a whole sector of problems that could better be solved by eliminating some solution that isn't working anymore. That's a big part of what humans as toolmakers and problem solvers do. What is problematic is how many people are taken in by the idea that new tools, new "stuff," are what is needed to address problems that can only be solved by humans acting humanly: with compassion, mercy, generosity, and wisdom. Instead, people devote increasing amounts of their time and psychic energy on gathering the wherewithal to have the stuff to solve the problems. Parents devote their time to having enough money for private school or other amenities for their children, leaving little time to be with their children and demonstrate how their children are personally important to them. Or people feel as though big charitable contributions make up for not taking the time to meet people's needs for human contact and compassion, not just their material needs.

As a species, we are too often arrogant and megalomaniacal in our self-interest. The consequences are coming home to roost. Our tools have resulted in various types of pollution and, as a consequence, the earth's atmosphere is warming alarmingly; we are already experiencing climate change, which, for practical purposes, can't be reversed, only ameliorated. Actions taken now can prevent the average temperature of the atmosphere from heating that much more, but it will be thousands of years before it actually cools. This has consequences for everything in our world. Climate change is not my area of expertise, but I do know one thing about something so catastrophically life-changing: We cannot afford to address this fearfully. And compassion is a very large part of why we need to act.

10. In July 2024, the computers enabling air travel and a lot of other important functions were completely knocked out for a day because of an error by CrowdStrike, a company paid to counter various malign internet attacks on their servers. It's ironic that the most effective malware attack wasn't an attack but a relatively simple mistake made by a company universally trusted to stop malware attacks. See Marshall, "Global CrowdStrike Outage."

Homo Technicus: The Tool User

Fearful people focus on themselves and act even more arrogantly than they would otherwise. Humans are not the only important things in the universe. Compassion is not limited to our close circle of family, friends, and associates—or our nation, or even humanity. Our care for humans must not become an excuse for further degrading environments and populations for other species. As *homo technicus*, we will always be using tools of many sorts to address our problems; it's what we do.[11]

When we are thoughtless and self-indulgent, we use tools as wholesale shortcuts, as solutions that disregard any consequences beyond the immediate problem at hand, conceived in the narrowest possible way.

A lot of people were surprised when, during the 2024 presidential campaign and in the months following, a substantial number of CEOs and major investors in so-called "tech" companies supported Donald Trump, after they had been widely perceived as liberals and reliable supporters of the Democratic Party. This perception was due to a belief, encouraged by the industry, that computers and digital technology in their essential structure carried a force that would build a new, more egalitarian future. On reflection, it's clear that the source of this belief is the aspirations of decades of science fiction writers, promoted by the public relations strategies of these companies. This development wasn't nearly as sudden as it appeared, nor should it have been surprising. Ultimately, computers and software are tools, the companies that develop and sell them are businesses, and their owners and executives make their choices in the same ways that the wealthy and powerful have always done. The most powerful tools in the history of humanity in the hands of a few powerful people cause powerful consequences in society, as we have seen in the effects of social media manipulation on elections and many other things. Some regard computers and the internet as a special category, with a special destiny independent of human judgment or mores. To the extent that this view becomes the norm, we become subject to those with the power to wield these tools.

Tools in the hands of fearful, anxious, selfish people become weapons of destruction that tear down not only opposing groups but our own society and the rest of the world. Tools should be something that make life easier for people, not the ultimate solution to all of society's ailments. Once we adjust our attitude toward our tools, we can use them to assist us to become the creative and compassionate people we were intended to be.

---

11. I'm currently typing this on a computer, for instance. Humans can't avoid being tool users.

This Idaho

FUNERAL HOMILY FOR DON KADEL, ST. DAVID'S EPISCOPAL CHURCH, CALDWELL, IDAHO, JUNE 26, 2005[1]

In this is love, not that we loved God but that he loved us.
—1 John 4:10

WE FLEW TO PORTLAND and drove to Caldwell. Coming up the Columbia Gorge in this late spring, the land and the water were so beautiful, so filled with life. It was so out of keeping with why we were making the journey—the death of my father. Somehow, I just can't be somber or sorrowful when surrounded by these western hills and deserts come to life with the rains and run-off of spring. I learned that from Don Kadel. The vigor and power of his life came in relation to the land—especially the wild and open land—in its beauty and the challenges it brought. He did know from a young age that "the grass withers and the flower fades."[2] Despite the poignancy of tales of locust plagues and dust infiltrating everything during his childhood in dust-bowl, Depression Kansas, what I always heard was the challenge to respond and adapt when the power of nature became a challenge. The exploits he recounted with the most relish usually involved serious discomfort or even danger—like when he was elk hunting with quite a bunch of

---

1. Readings: Isa 40:6–9, 1 John 4:7–11.
2. Isa 40:8.

pack animals in twenty degrees below zero weather and tried to ford a large creek, which was freezing from the bottom up.

The mountains, the deserts, and the open land were Dad's great joy. Equally was being and sharing with people—with family and friends. I know my father's love more by what he did than by what he said—by including, teaching, or protecting me—I mostly remember his anger only when he was standing up for one of his children. Not that he didn't talk—he would tell stories for hours—filled with his mischievous sense of humor.

To my knowledge, the last time Don Kadel was in this church was for my ordination twenty-four years ago. He supported me, even though he couldn't understand why I would want to undertake such a crazy path. As far as I could tell, the only really useful thing about church for Don was that it made the mountains a little less crowded on Sundays. He actually made few remarks about religion, but the one thing that I remember him saying with some feeling was that there was a noticeable number of members of some religious groups who would make a big show of their strict principles of behavior and then, the next day, turn around and cheat, even steal from others, with no conscience about it.

So, this brings us to the lesson:

> In this is love, not that we loved God but that he loved us. (1 John 4:10)

Love of God is not proven in pious words or in self-justification. Love is first founded in God, the creator. The creator of all that is, especially this land we call home—this Idaho. The love is God's love for every human being, for Don Kadel and for each of us. As a theologian, I learned to appreciate the forms and power of words. But that can also lead in false directions. For as the New Testament lesson reminds us, "Everyone who loves is born of God and knows God"(1 John 4:7).

Don Kadel was clearly one of those, generous of his spirit and his substance: a loving husband to his wife Bernice; a loving father to his daughter Nancy, his son Brad, and to me; grandfather to Rachel, Lisa, Maggie, and Julliana; great-grandfather to Isabel; caring brother; loyal friend.

After the service at the reception at the Elks, we will have an opportunity to share remembrances of him.

Remember:

> No one has ever seen God. If we love one another, God lives in us.
> And his love is perfected in us. (1 John 4:12)

Let us thank God for the life of Donald Milburn Kadel and love one another.

3

The World Where I Grew Up

Oddly enough the overriding sensation I got looking at the Earth was: My God, that little thing is so fragile out there.
—Astronaut Michael Collins, Apollo 11 pilot[1]

I WAS BORN IN Idaho, and, though I've lived in and around New York City for a good portion of my adult life now, there are still many things about me that reflect that part of the world where people still think in terms of manifest destiny and taming the frontier. It's America at its quintessential best and worst, especially when it comes to its racist past and present.

I'm the direct descendent of the settlers of the American West. My great grandmother on my mother's side, Anna Irene Smith, was born in December of 1881, shortly after her parents took a covered wagon from the rail head at Ogden, Utah, and started a homestead near Council, Idaho. I remember my great-grandma's eightieth birthday party, held in the dining room of our house in Caldwell. The cake was decorated with a map of Idaho with icing stars for all the places in the Snake River Valley where she'd lived. Mom had put eighty candles on the cake, and when Great-Grandma blew them out, her wispy white hair caught fire. There was much consternation, but no actual harm. Great-Grandma's older sister came from California for

---

1. Carlowicz, "Eagle Takes Off."

the occasion. Mom remarked later that the sister had first come to Idaho on a covered wagon and her last time was on an airplane.[2]

We were very proud to be children of the pioneers who had opened up the empty land of the West, made the deserts bloom with abundant crops, and built prosperous towns and cities. At least, that's what we were told, and that's what we believed when I was a kid. There was no population of Native Americans who were at all visible nearby, and the sagebrush country beyond the reach of the irrigation systems seemed pretty uninhabitable. Of course, we didn't really stop to think about how that town of Council got its name. It was in the little valley where the various bands of indigenous people gathered to trade and socialize every year, which Americans called a "council."

And the Ward Massacre Memorial was very near our town. In 1854, a small group of about six wagons was traveling toward Fort Boise, which was at the confluence of the Boise and Snake Rivers, about forty-five miles from the current city of Boise. They were confronted by some indigenous men, probably Shoshonis or Paiutes, who wanted to trade for a horse. The negotiations didn't go well; one of the indigenous men took the horse and started to ride off, and one of the members of the Ward party shot and killed him. Soon, a large band attacked the Ward party and killed eighteen people, including all the women and children. The descriptions of the massacre are quite brutal and appeared to be mostly based on the accounts of two young teenaged boys who escaped after being wounded. Prior to 1853, relations between the wagon-train emigrants and the local indigenous people were mostly peaceful, characterized by trade and mutual assistance. But the huge increase in travelers, who let their stock overgraze the grasslands, frustrated the native peoples who could see they were being exploited. The Ward Massacre wasn't the first attack on wagon trains, but after it happened, the Snake River Indians became so hostile that the Hudson Bay Company closed its trading posts at Fort Boise and Fort Hall and left the region altogether. Travel on the Oregon Trail was greatly curtailed because emigrants had to be accompanied by soldiers. In 1862, however, large gold deposits were found in Idaho, and the Snake River Valley became an important destination for treasure seekers and their suppliers, so travel picked right up again.

As an Idahoan, I saw both sides of the conflict. I was taken as a kid to the Ward Massacre Memorial. No one knows exactly where the massacre

---

2. It might have been a jet, I can't remember.

occurred, but this was at the place where the Army erected gallows to hang four men they claimed had participated in the massacre the year before—the gallows were left standing after the executions to serve as a warning.[3] There was no sign of the gallows by the 1960s, just a large stone with a plaque with the names of the dead erected by the Daughters of the American Revolution. I mostly remember it as a dry spot and hard to find. But it confirmed the "cowboys and Indians" view of westward expansion that I was taught at school and permeated popular culture.

Years later, when I was doing a chaplaincy internship in Boise, I got to know a patient who was hospitalized long-term because of an infection consequent to a failed knee replacement. She was Shoshoni/Paiute and came from the Duck Valley Indian Reservation. Unlike the bountiful lands on the Snake River plain, Duck Valley is on the worst leftover land in the high desert on the Idaho-Nevada border. Those who live there are deeply impoverished, shunted to the side by the same people who overgrazed their land in the 1850s. Because of the lack of water, the patient had to carry water from a well some distance from her house from the 1950s onward. By the 1970s, her knees were worn out. Knee replacements were new and unreliable at that time, and slipshod post-operative care resulted in a terrible chronic infection. Hardly anyone bothered to do the isolation routine required to enter her room; typically, the nurse would stand at the entrance of the room and ask her if she needed anything. So, I was about the only person who actually visited with her during my weeks on the orthopedic ward. In southwest Idaho, Native Americans were truly invisible. Most people thought they didn't exist among us at all.

My great-grandmother's husband, James Fields Chaney, was the only son of his mother, who died when he was very young. As a teenager, James traveled with his father, bringing a large string of mules from Missouri to the mining camps in Idaho. His father became a prosperous farmer and banker in Middleton, Idaho, but James was largely alienated from his father, mostly because he didn't get along with his second wife who preferred her own children. He started farming on his own but went bankrupt and finally settled on a small ranch during the 1920s, just over the state line in Oregon by the banks of the Snake River. James' eighteen-year-old son, Horace Chaney, had to sign the papers to buy the ranch because the bankruptcy

---

3. The best source for material on the Oregon Trail before the Civil War is Unruh, *Plains Across*.

The World Where I Grew Up

precluded my great-grandfather from buying property in his own name. It was a hard and not very prosperous life.

James' son, my grandpa Horace, was a cowboy, looking like a much bigger man when mounted on a horse than when he was walking.[4] A group shared a grazing lease in the Owyhees, twenty or thirty miles from the ranch. He obtained some of his horses through wild horse roundups that were held from time to time. My mother, Bernice, or Berni as she was known all her life, saw nothing romantic about the grind of work on the farm and left for college as soon as she graduated from high school at fifteen.[5] She had a Welsh pony, but she wasn't interested in the outdoors or horses. Instead, she would wrap the reins around the saddle horn and let the pony walk to the school on its own while she read her books. One summer while she was in college, Berni worked as a cowboy on her father's ranch, living at the cattle camp, wrangling cattle, and branding newborn calves. Her father was always anxious about money—I remember him constantly ranting about inflation, likening the situation in the late 1960s to Weimar, Germany, when it took a wheelbarrow full of banknotes to buy a loaf of bread. In 1968, he was a precinct committeeman for George Wallace's American Independent Party.

Years later, when my mom talked about working with some idealistic young people who wanted to buy remote rural property and "live off the land," she would shake her head and tell me, "They just don't understand that if you are raising all your own food and managing the land, you don't have time or energy to do any of the things that they value, like reading, art, or environmental activism."[6] Being descended from pioneers was perhaps a point of pride, but Mom, at least, didn't regard it with romantic nostalgia.

My father's family were, as Woody Guthrie put it, "dust bowl refugees." My grandfather, a Marine Corps veteran of World War I and an orphan, had purchased a farm in north central Kansas where he and Grandma started their family that eventually included twelve children. As drought came, locusts ate the wheat in the fields and even the paint off the house,

---

4. I also have a long torso and short inseam, but Grandpa looked like John Wayne when he was riding. I don't think that applies to me.

5. The two-room Big Bend schoolhouse made it necessary for the teacher to let Berni do the work of two grades simultaneously, since she always had the make-work done ahead of everyone else and was asking questions during the other class's instruction time anyway.

6. That's what she said. While there are examples of people "living off the land" who do some of these things, it's worth looking into the extent to which they have other sources of income or assistance in working the land.

and the air filled with dust that infiltrated everything. Grandma put damp washcloths over the kids' faces as they slept so they could breathe and laid the plates upside down when she set the table so dust wouldn't coat them before the meal began. And then the crops failed. Grandpa had to go on "relief," which, at that time, meant working all day on road building in exchange for commodities. My father never allowed lamb to be cooked in our home because the meat in those commodities allotments was canned mutton, which was often rancid. The smell of it cooking reminded him of his father's humiliation and made him nauseous.

They held on until 1939. The bank had foreclosed on the farm about a year earlier, allowing them to stay and work the farm in exchange for paying the property tax. In October, there was a farm sale where they auctioned off the farm and all its equipment. The family headed out to Idaho in a Chevrolet sedan and a farm truck with their personal belongings and what was then eleven children. When they stopped in Wyoming at a motel, Grandpa counted out all his money: $110.00. Uncle Lloyd, the oldest boy, said, "But there's more coming from the farm sale, isn't there?"

"No, that's it," Grandpa said.

Grandpa never owned a full-time farm again. He became a parts man for a farm implements dealership. And many of his children worked for businesses adjacent to agriculture, because that was Idaho at that time. Overall, my father's family was much more prosperous than my mom's family, who stayed in farming to a large extent.

People live their lives, develop their beliefs, care for their families, and find their loves in the context where they find themselves. Mostly, they believe what they are told, unless it contradicts their personal experience, and they value those who are close to them. My family enjoyed one another, particularly my dad and his brothers. If anything, the hardships and poverty of their childhood brought them closer together as adults when they lived in relative prosperity. There certainly was casual racism in my family though; except for my mom's father, I never noticed any particular ire or resentment among them. As sons and daughters of the pioneers, they lived in a land of plenty and, for the most, part enjoyed it. I doubt that I would have the same impression if I returned home to Idaho during current times.

American slavery and racism, the genocide of indigenous North Americans, and European colonialism are all of a piece. While it is true that all manner of peoples in all sorts of times and places have had conflicts and wars, fighting over control of land and enslaving one another, there's something quite distinct and particularly disturbing about the project of European and white American colonialism in all its manifestations.[7]

It is not just the scale or success that differentiates European colonialism from other conflicts between peoples and cultures. There is a major spiritual problem. It is the problem of using the image and teaching of the one who exemplifies humility and the care and healing of oppressed people to justify naked use of power against other groups for the enrichment of the powerful and arrogant. The progress of this is complicated and I'll leave the writing of medieval and modern history to others. However, it certainly can be seen in the Crusades and in the dividing of the world between Portugal and Spain by Pope Alexander VI. In any case, there is a great contrast between the spirituality of western Europe in the late medieval and early modern periods and that of Patriarch John Chrysostom of Constantinople (d. 407), who would take the wealthy to task in his sermons with great regularity.

A major factor in this change is the increasingly abstract way in which Christ was regarded. Despite the orthodox doctrine of Jesus having both a divine and a human nature, Christ was primarily regarded as God with no qualification—thus God and King. Those seeking any human aspect of the divine were referred to the Virgin Mary. And while it is possible to find subtle and nuanced writing about Christ among medieval theologians, the bottom line for most Christians in power, and most preachers and teachers, was to attribute to Jesus the perquisites and entitlements of worldly rulers, which resulted in a church that was run like a worldly kingdom. This is a phenomenon of most ages, but it arguably reached its apotheosis with the splendor and venality of the Renaissance popes of the fifteenth century. One would think that the great disruption of the Protestant Reformation in the next century would have fixed all that, but insofar as the uncritical sanctification of worldly power was concerned, it certainly didn't.

This is not to say that there were no voices from the Middle Ages that didn't speak out against the church's accrual of wealth and power. For instance, St. Francis of Assisi taught about Christ's love for the poor and Jesus' own poverty. But those in ecclesiastical and secular power made sure that this message was perceived as calling on parishioners to give to private charity, rather than church leaders giving up their perquisites.

As Europeans' technological and military power increased, their adherence to Christ, the All-Good, All-Loving, the Only Way, Truth, and Life,

7. Graeber, *Dawn of Everything*, 493–526.

was translated in their mindset as meaning that their culture represented the only real civilization. They believed that entitled—and commanded—them to bring not only the message of Jesus but their way of life to all the world. This became the conviction not only of those who were religious but, even more so, for those who definitely were not. The rationale for the triumph of "civilization"—now not even qualified by "Christian"—became the imperative for European politicians and political theorists and philosophers in general, no matter what their views on Christianity or religion might be.[8]

Humility is hard to find among Europeans intent on civilizing the world. Though I think that some of the missionaries cared deeply for the welfare of the people they were sent to civilize and convert, there were many who did not. Jesus has always been there—teaching the Sermon on the Mount, healing, casting out demons, and calling the sanctimonious to account. But the pathway to success in church or "Christian civilization" has been to accept the gloss of the powerful—that what Jesus did really has nothing to do with what ordinary people should do and that his salvation is entirely otherworldly; the work of establishing Christendom in good order is more important than following the example of Jesus. Jesus is thus fused with the self-serving agenda of the powerful, and the result is that many people ended up misunderstanding faith as meaning "civilized."

The collective impact of this on the church was to blunt and impair its spirituality. And it gave carte blanche for the secular and political realm to exercise all power and violence to take over lands and subjugate their people. After all, they were establishing the kingdom of Christ! Or, for the more secular, the destiny of their obviously superior civilization with its rationality and goodness required its full and absolute implementation. The sanctimony that Jesus so harshly criticized became the uniting principle for the Western world and its colonialism.

The world reached a point—ironically, the point was roughly when colonialism was almost fully triumphant—when it could no longer bear it. People saw through it. Especially those from colonized countries, or those descended from the enslaved or the disappeared ones. The last to appreciate this are those of us who are white, settlers, or children of settlers, and those who thrive on the legacy of the wholesale exploitation of the world and its people. Many modern-day conflicts are the result of those colonized people

---

8. Graeber, *Dawn of Everything*, 1–77. The first two chapters are takedowns of Rousseau and the rest of Enlightenment philosophy in this regard.

asserting their own dignity and rights—and the costs entailed in changing the status quo. The resolution of these conflicts is not simple; it is the work of at least another generation.

The spiritual aspect of this problem is pride. The Greeks called it hubris, while the medieval theologians identified pride as the deadliest of the seven deadly sins and the root of all of them. I'm not talking about the pride that is satisfaction with a job well done or in seeing one's child achieve important milestones. This pride is the arrogance that chooses itself as the measure of all things, that seeks and asserts its superiority over others rather than building the common good and celebrating the triumphs of others. It would be a mistake to believe that there has been no compassion or humility or selflessness among colonists or settlers. Had that been the case, Western civilization would have collapsed entirely long ago. But the grandiosity of Europe and the United States believing that their destiny was to control the entire world was manifest in the most prideful of all the ways of empire. I grew up believing in "American exceptionalism"—that somehow, the United States was a "city on a hill" where we lived by principle and generosity to other peoples.

I was naïve and thought it was a fact—as opposed to a propaganda platform. It took a while for me to start seeing that it often came along with a lack of generosity or outright exploitation. I was young enough at the start of the Vietnam War that it took me a while to understand what we were being told was a lie. Believing in American exceptionalism, I regarded such things as aberrations that could be fixed—that we could/should/would be that city on a hill if we just were American enough. It took time to realize that American exceptionalism is a perfect example of hubris—of inflated self-regard and blindness to obvious facts. It took much longer to recognize that the whole thing was a construct of self-justification for white Americans.

The default spiritual approach of white Americans has a severely defective view of grace[9]—mostly because they refuse to see the depth of the sin and harms that they have caused and are implicated in. We are human,

---

9. It's tempting to call it Pelagianism, after Augustine's controversies over the teachings of an English monk named Pelagius regarding whether human effort rather than grace can perfect human behavior. But it's unlikely that Augustine was being fair to Pelagius and the naïve, nascent spirituality widely distributed to the American public (sometimes called Therapeutic Moralistic Deism, as Christian Smith and Melissa Denton described it in their book *Soul Searching*) doesn't share all the elements of the heresy as defined, and is largely uncritical and unaware of theological arguments in any case.

we deserve compassion and grace; but it's necessary to live in the real world, including our own culpability, for that grace to have any meaning. It's one thing to enjoy the heritage of the pioneers, breathing in the aroma of the sagebrush desert and watching the sunset over the western mountains. It is another thing altogether to be blind to the Shoshoni and Paiute and forget our part in their suffering and privation over such a long time.

The resolution and healing of the damage inflicted by colonialism, slavery, and genocide is a long-term project. Quick fixes and panaceas won't bring it any closer. There are a thousand, or tens of thousands of, important things that can be done that can contribute to healing. These must be done. But fundamentally, it involves giving up our pride and becoming compassionate, decent people. That's actually a bigger challenge than a political program with defined policies to be implemented over the next few years—it amounts to a permanent change for all of us.

On Asparagus and Being a Neighbor

A SERMON PREACHED AT THE CHURCH OF ST. MARK'S IN THE BOWERY, NEW YORK CITY ON FEBRUARY 23, 2014[1]

When you reap the harvest of your land, you shall not reap to the very edges of your field, or gather the gleanings of your harvest. You shall not strip your vineyard bare, or gather the fallen grapes of your vineyard; you shall leave them for the poor and the alien.

—Leviticus 19:9–10

The lesson from Leviticus today is from what scholars call the Holiness Code. It's a set of instructions of how the people of Israel are to be a holy people, dedicated to God. There are paragraphs that talk about right worship and ritual purity, but just as much the commands of God about being a holy people are about ordinary everyday things. Things that were not special to the Israelites, but were simply things that were expected of upstanding people: "You shall not defraud your neighbor, you shall not steal; and you shall not keep for yourself the wages of a laborer until the morning," for instance.

The text I quoted is one of those. It defines gleaning. In our urban context, we might not be familiar with it, or, if we know about it, we might be inclined to romanticize it or think it's a particularly religious thing. I grew up in Idaho, prosperous farming country. For over forty years, my father

---

1. Lectionary readings: Lev 19:12, 9–18; 1 Cor 3:10–11, 16–23; Matt 5:38–48.

sold insurance to farmers, mostly to cover their farming business. When I was very little, my earliest memories are of living in a little house in the countryside. My parents were young and just starting out, and they were renting what had been a "hired-man's house" from a prosperous farmer down the road. Sometimes I would walk with my mom along the country road. The banks of the irrigation ditches were allowed to grow wild with sunflowers and weeds and grass.

Birds would take shelter there and sometimes build their nests. The ditch banks belonged to the farmers' fields, but nobody particularly cared what you did on the ditch banks as long as you didn't divert the water.[2] One of the things that we did, even long after we moved to town, was to hunt for wild asparagus on the ditch banks. This was a kind of gleaning; you didn't have to be poor or on the margins of society. In the spring, lots of people would drive slowly along country roads until they spied a little colony of the vegetable. It was fun, it was good to eat, and commercially grown asparagus was almost unknown in Idaho at that time. The thing is, the boundaries of the fields were more or less necessary waste space. You couldn't efficiently harvest crops out to the very edges, and those margins became, in effect, part of the commons which people could share, if they followed the unwritten rules. Allowing this and other kinds of gleaning wasn't seen as particularly virtuous or holy, it was simply part of being relaxed neighbors.

So, what's the deal in the Leviticus passage? The most important part of being holy is leading a decent, common-sense, human life. But there's always someone who wants to game that—to scrape just a little closer to the edge of the field, or even enhance their relative position by making someone else's life just a little harder, even if there is no positive gain in doing that. Why send your slaves out to rake up all the loose grapes that have fallen to the ground? It nets little or nothing. Certainly not compared to the benefit of being a good neighbor.

Jesus was teaching in a different historical period,[3] a thousand years or more after the time depicted in the Leviticus passage. In those days of the Roman occupation, people could be compelled to carry burdens for the army, for instance, and society was more complex with more towns

---

2. Shortly after I preached this sermon, I spoke with my mother on the phone. She had read the sermon and reminded me that now, the farmers in Idaho have modified their irrigation and harvesting practices and plant clear out to the property line, eliminating ditch banks, wildlife habitat, and anything resembling gleaning.

3. The Gospel reading for this Sunday was Matt 5:38–48.

and cities. But Jesus' concern is the same—he didn't want people to try to establish rights over others just to assert some kind of advantage over them. Jesus uses extreme imagery of radical nonresistance and absolute generosity, but that's not to establish a new game with higher stakes—some sort of all or nothing situation. Jesus is challenging us to give up on self-justification based on playing around with rules and rights, to pay attention, and become real neighbors.

Neighbors are people who you share things with and that you have to get along with in order to have a functioning community. It doesn't mean that they are people you like, agree with, or even share tastes or cultural preferences. The more complex the society, the more complex is the question of our neighbors.

One response to this complexity is to define more clearly and tightly who neighbors might be. Corporations have always existed for the benefit of their owners, the stockholders, but in the past couple of decades, this has been pushed to its logical and most efficient limit (as philosophers would say, its *reductio ad absurdum*): no neighborly action is justified unless it can be demonstrated that it enhances shareholder profit. Some try to limit the complexity of who they deal with based on culture, ethnicity, visa status, or political allegiance. And this is not true of only one end of the political spectrum. It is easy to seek out enclaves of like-minded friends and to shut out and ignore those that one assumes might think or say things that would make you uncomfortable.

But Jesus says, "You have heard that it was said, 'You shall love your neighbor and hate your enemy.' But I say to you, Love your enemies and pray for those who persecute you, so that you may be children of your Father in heaven" (Matt 5:44–45).

It takes great courage to take Jesus at his word and to face our complex society with openness and generosity of spirit. It can be costly, as it was for Jesus, to love those who aren't your sisters and brothers, but it is really the only way to healing and holiness. As the passage from Leviticus ends, "You shall not take vengeance or bear a grudge against any of your people, but you shall love your neighbor as yourself: I am the Lord" (Lev 19:18).

4

The Heart of the Text

When we look at ancient writings, especially the Bible, the most important part of the text is usually in the middle. Most modern styles of writing don't approach topics that way. News articles, for example, start by giving the basics of the story: who, what, when, where, and why, followed by a paragraph that elaborates briefly on the first. Then, there are further paragraphs fleshing out the story, with the most relevant or current information first, then relevant older background information.[1]

But it is far more common in biblical texts for the most important part to be in the center, set up with context or even disclaimers, and then continuing in a more or less symmetrical fashion with the implications of the central message. This is the text of Psalm 1 as it appears in the *Book of Common Prayer of the Episcopal Church*.[2] This psalm serves as the introduction to the collection.

> Happy are they who have not walked in the counsel of the wicked,
> nor lingered in the way of sinners, nor sat in the seats of the scornful!
> Their delight is in the law of the LORD,
> and they meditate on his law day and night.
> They are like trees planted by streams of water,
> bearing fruit in due season, with leaves that do not wither;

---

1. The generally accepted reason for why this style evolved the way it did was because, when newspapers were print-only, the typesetter needed to be able to cut off to arrange stories in the available column inches.

2. The book of Psalms is a compilation for the worship of the second temple in Jerusalem, the one built after the return from the Babylonian exile.

everything they do shall prosper.
It is not so with the wicked;
they are like chaff which the wind blows away.
Therefore the wicked shall not stand upright when judgment comes,
nor the sinner in the council of the righteous.
For the LORD knows the way of the righteous,
but the way of the wicked is doomed. (Ps 1)[3]

"Like a tree planted by streams of water, bearing fruit in due season" (Ps 1:3 RSV). The heart of this psalm is not about the wicked; it's about the foundation of life found in the law of the Lord. The literary term for this is chiasm, referring to the Greek letter "chi," which is shaped like an X or cross. It has nothing to do with the cross of Christ—except when a Christian commentator wants to riff on the concept. In this construct, a sentence, a paragraph, or an entire book, flows toward the center where it crosses and then flows back out to the edge. Scholars often get into highly technical debates over just how much symmetry there is and where the true center of the chiasm actually occurs, and that's fine for scholars. But it's enough to know that ancient literature contains so much use of chiasm that it's pretty clear it wasn't a mere device: it's a fundamental way this literature was structured.

The primary Scriptures of Judaism are the five books of Moses, called the Torah—the Law, or perhaps, the Teaching. There are other Scriptures that have authority, but it is the Torah that is the primary focus of Jewish worship, and interpretation of its contents are the foundation of the distinctive Jewish practices, like dietary laws and Sabbath observance.

---

3 The translation I've cited in the text uses the plural instead of the singular in several places because of an effort to use inclusive language. But it may help interpret the text to see it in the singular as in the Revised Standard Version:

> Blessed is the man who walks not in the counsel of the wicked,
> nor stands in the way of sinners, nor sits in the seat of scoffers;
> but his delight is in the law of the LORD,
> and on his law he meditates day and night.
> He is like a tree planted by streams of water,
> that yields its fruit in its season, and its leaf does not wither.
> In all that he does, he prospers.
> The wicked are not so,
> but are like chaff which the wind drives away.
> Therefore the wicked will not stand in the judgment,
> nor sinners in the congregation of the righteous;
> for the LORD knows the way of the righteous,
> but the way of the wicked will perish.

Taken as a whole, the Pentateuch has a chiastic structure. The books on the outside, Genesis and Deuteronomy, begin with creation and end with the preparation to enter the promised land. Next up, as we progress toward the center from the beginning and end, are books of the law—Exodus, which recounts deliverance from Egypt, and Numbers, based on Israel's time in the desert. In the center is Leviticus.[4] Leviticus is primarily a liturgical book. It gives instructions to the priests on how to conduct sacrifices. These sacrifices—the system of sacrifices, devotional acts, and rules governing eating, sexual behavior, and so on—define the relationship of the people with God, the source and ruler of all things. Praise, communion with God and the community, and repentance and expiation of sin were the fundamental reasons for different types of sacrifice. Rules governing foods, aspects of health and sexual behavior, and purification from ritual impurity defined the boundaries of the community and relations within it.

At the center of the book of Leviticus is what scholars call the Holiness Code. It defines how the holy people of God live. This excerpt defines its purpose:

> The Lord spoke to Moses, saying:
> Speak to the people of Israel and say to them:
> *I am the Lord your God.*
> You shall not do as they do in the land of Egypt, where you lived, and you shall not do as they do in the land of Canaan, to which I am bringing you. You shall not follow their statutes.
> My ordinances you shall observe and my statutes you shall keep, following them:
> *I am the Lord your God.*
> You shall keep my statutes and my ordinances;
> by doing so one shall live:
> *I am the Lord.* (Lev 18:1–5, emphasis added)

The heart of the Holiness Code and the heart of Leviticus is chapter nineteen. In form, it is a series of commands interspersed with the refrain "I am the Lord your God," or "I am the Lord." In Hebrew, the word "Lord" is YHWH, the name of God, which ceased to be pronounced at some point in

---

4. This is, of course, tremendously simplified. Each of these books has a complex history of compilation and editing and contains traditions, laws, and narrative from different sources and times. It's most likely that these books took their current form during the Babylonian exile or within the period following it. Nonetheless, I'm convinced that this overall chiastic structure is intended.

The Heart of the Text

the Second Temple period.[5] These commands overlap with the Ten Commandments and share the form somewhat, but are dedicated to defining the behavior of the holy people. The code emphasizes that this is about specific loyalty to a specific named God and that this holy people's practices are different either from those of Egypt, where they once lived, or from those of Canaan, where they were to go and settle. At the very heart of this, however, are these commands:

> When you reap the harvest of your land, you shall not reap to the very edges of your field, or gather the gleanings of your harvest. You shall not strip your vineyard bare, or gather the fallen grapes of your vineyard; you shall leave them for the poor and the alien: I am the Lord your God. (Lev 19:9–10)
>
> You shall not defraud your neighbor; you shall not steal; and you shall not keep for yourself the wages of a laborer until morning. You shall not revile the deaf or put a stumbling-block before the blind; you shall fear your God: I am the Lord. (Lev 19:13–14)
>
> You shall not render an unjust judgement; you shall not be partial to the poor or defer to the great: with justice you shall judge your neighbor. You shall not go around as a slanderer among your people, and you shall not profit by the blood of your neighbor: I am the Lord. (Lev 19:15–16)
>
> You shall not hate in your heart anyone of your kin; you shall reprove your neighbor, or you will incur guilt yourself. You shall not take vengeance or bear a grudge against any of your people, but you shall love your neighbor as yourself: I am the Lord. (Lev 19:17–18)
>
> When an alien resides with you in your land, you shall not oppress the alien. The alien who resides with you shall be to you as the citizen among you; you shall love the alien as yourself, for you were aliens in the land of Egypt: I am the Lord your God. (Lev 19:33–34)
>
> You shall not cheat in measuring length, weight, or quantity. You shall have honest balances, honest weights, an honest *ephah*, and an honest *hin*: I am the Lord your God, who brought you out of the

---

5. The form of commands followed by a refrain is a common liturgical practice. I can remember as a child in the Episcopal Church having the Holy Communion service during Lent begin with the priest reading the Ten Commandments. After each one, the congregation would intone, to John Merbecke's tune (701 in the *Hymnal 1940*): "Lord, have mercy upon us, and incline our hearts to keep this law."

land of Egypt. You shall keep all my statutes and all my ordinances, and observe them: I am the Lord. (Lev 19:35–37)

The focus of this chapter at the heart of Leviticus is on justice and fair dealing, emphasizing particularly the poor and aliens dwelling in the community. In the very place where the distinctiveness of Israel from other nations is most important, where being holy separate and apart from other nations is the theme, justice and fairness for those who aren't part of that holy people is emphasized. Why is this? I see two aspects of this that are related but also poles apart. First is ordinary decency. The duty and practice of hospitality was widespread in the ancient Near East. That included welcoming strangers and treating fairly those who peacefully settled within your community. It is what decent people did. Certainly, the people of Israel and the drafters of Leviticus regarded their community as at least decent.

The other aspect is that fairness and equal-handed treatment of all people was at the core of Israel's identity. Prophets had a particular role in Israel that is really distinct from what we see elsewhere. We have writings of prophets and prophetic traditions that date from well before the Assyrian invasion of the northern kingdom of Israel in 722 BCE, or the destruction of the temple in Jerusalem, and the Babylonian exile in 587 BCE. There are plenty of indications in the other scriptural texts that prophets like Amos or Hosea weren't the first to show up on the scene. For example, Nathan was a prophet in the court of King David centuries earlier. These prophets were characterized by their willingness to criticize the leaders and people of Israel, as well as foreign nations, to hold them to account in the name of YHWH, their God. Fairness to the poor and the oppressed is a constant theme in the prophets' texts. Naïve or simple universalism is not characteristic of the prophets but rather the belief that their God triumphs over all and demands justice and fairness for all. Being a holy people means being dedicated to this God and this justice.

Leviticus combines a demand to "just be decent, for God's sake!" with a call to be a people particularly dedicated, as were the prophets, to God, who values the lowliest and most rejected equally with kings and high priests.

The much-misunderstood "Parable of the Good Samaritan" (Luke 10:25–37) is an interpretation of this chapter of Leviticus. It's not just that the lawyer who's debating Jesus quotes part of verse 18. The entire discussion of "who is my neighbor?" and the parable are about the role and treatment of aliens and sojourners by the people of Israel. The estrangement between

Samaritans and Jews was bitter.[6] Samaritans were viewed with suspicion as aliens and idolators by Jews who believed that they had intermarried with non-Israelites. Jesus' interpretation of Leviticus 19 to include the Samaritans as neighbors was a perfectly reasonable exegesis of a well-known passage of the Torah. It's the kind of argument that rabbis had with one another on a regular basis. At the same time, it was provocative and illustrates the increasing tension between Jesus and other Pharisees.

Religious texts are read in different ways by people depending on what they are seeking. Often, these differences are honest and in good faith. But the reason for the existence of every religious text is to say something that transcends human self-interest, including talk about God, the love of God, the will of God, obligations for generosity, and detachment from worldly goods.[7] Rightly understood, Scripture can make people uncomfortable precisely because their own behavior is out of step with its meaning. It's not uncommon for some to avoid this discomfort by misinterpreting these texts and putting forth bad-faith readings of them.

The politicized evangelicalism in the United States that passes itself off to gullible nonbelievers as "the only true Christianity" completely ignores the heart of the teaching of Moses and the heart of the teaching of Jesus. These few verses at the center of Leviticus are only a sample of the theme running throughout all of Scripture, both Jewish and Christian, that the poor are beloved by God and that the worst of God's wrath is for those who mistreat the poor, the widow, the sojourner, and those otherwise marginalized. Mary Beard, a historian of ancient Rome who otherwise is not very sympathetic with the church, described the Romans' puzzlement with early Christians:

---

6. I discuss some of the details of this in chapter five. The parable only appears in Luke, which I believe is the latest of the Gospels. Its author notes his methodology of gathering and evaluating all the traditions available at the time to make a coherent and authoritative record. The positive portrayal of the Samaritan may reflect this later time when Christians and Jews had become hostile to one another, and there are some indications of Christians making inroads with Samaritans in that period. In any case, the modern use of Samaritan to mean any person who intervenes to help out in a difficult situation, especially out on a road, doesn't reflect what was happening in that region at that time.

7. In different religious traditions, the role of God or gods, or even the existence of God, differs tremendously. Many forms of Buddhism are nontheist. Popular gods and demons may be acknowledged but are regarded as part of the world that is ultimately to be transcended. Others, such as Confucianism, may appear to Western eyes as simply ethical systems but in fact point to maintenance of the underlying structure of reality, which isn't subject to human choice. The myriad of gods of Hinduism typically, in Indian philosophy and spirituality, point beyond themselves to an underlying structure beyond the transitory and toward release from the wheel of rebirth.

What is more, some Christians were preaching values that threatened to overturn some of the most fundamental Greco-Roman assumptions about the nature of the world and of the people within it: that poverty, for example, was good; or that the body was to be tamed or rejected rather than cared for. All these factors help to explain the worries, confusion and hostility of Pliny and others like him.[8]

The various strands of evangelicalism, particularly the "prosperity gospel" and "dominionist" groups seek instead to valorize being wealthy and are actively hostile to anyone who might truly be described as a stranger or poor. Instead, they claim, in the most self-pitying ways, that they are the ones being persecuted. They prioritize gaining political power so they can dominate others, enforcing a Christian polity that has no room for anyone advocating for strangers, which can include anyone outside their clique. Their values resemble those of the Romans more than those of Jesus. It is true that there have been many Christians, including clergy and theologians, who have been enamored with power and used it against others, including the poor. Few have been as bald about it, without even lip service to the text of Jesus, the prophets, and the core of Leviticus, as the current crop of evangelicals, however.

Christians, especially evangelicals who emphasize conversion as a prime doctrine, focus on the process and forms of "accepting Jesus" and forget about the poor, the alien, or anyone outside their group. Ironically, this type of focus on Jesus leads people to behave in exactly the ways that Jesus most criticized. The whole of scripture is very concerned not with inner inclinations but with how people treat one another. The Torah and the prophets are very aware that people will be unfaithful to their social commitments. Abuse by the powerful within the community of spiritual or material privilege is the greatest sacrilege; the judgment of God is most intense for kings, unfaithful priests, and false prophets. The most radical statements of John the Baptist and Jesus are really just reminders to people to uphold their social obligations, be decent people, and to stop exploiting others.

It's often asserted that Christianity is a "religion of the heart," or that it is more important to have the right internal attitude than to be concerned with doing things that change how things are for other people. I want to look at the text that is most frequently cited as the source of this belief. The fifth chapter of the Gospel of Matthew is the heart of Jesus' Sermon on the Mount:

---

8. Beard, *SPQR*, 519–20.

> You have heard that it was said to those of ancient times, "You shall not murder"; and "whoever murders shall be liable to judgement." But I say to you that if you are angry with a brother or sister, you will be liable to judgement; and if you insult a brother or sister, you will be liable to the council; and if you say, "You fool," you will be liable to the hell of fire. So when you are offering your gift at the altar, if you remember that your brother or sister has something against you, leave your gift there before the altar and go; first be reconciled to your brother or sister, and then come and offer your gift. Come to terms quickly with your accuser while you are on the way to court with him, or your accuser may hand you over to the judge, and the judge to the guard, and you will be thrown into prison. Truly I tell you, you will never get out until you have paid the last penny.
>
> You have heard that it was said, "You shall not commit adultery." But I say to you that everyone who looks at a woman with lust has already committed adultery with her in his heart. If your right eye causes you to sin, tear it out and throw it away; it is better for you to lose one of your members than for your whole body to be thrown into hell. And if your right hand causes you to sin, cut it off and throw it away; it is better for you to lose one of your members than for your whole body to go into hell.
>
> It was also said, "Whoever divorces his wife, let him give her a certificate of divorce." But I say to you that anyone who divorces his wife, except on the ground of unchastity, causes her to commit adultery; and whoever marries a divorced woman commits adultery. (Matt 5:21–32)

This has often led Christians to interpret Jesus as offering a "spiritualized" or "internalized" interpretation of the Law. But in each of these cases, Jesus is criticizing behavior that purports to be allowed under the Law but damages individuals and the community, subverting the purpose of that very law. In the passage about anger, the word translated as "you fool" is actually "*raka*," a crude Aramaic insult left untranslated in the Greek. It means something more like rubbish or worthless, somewhat cruder than saying, "You loser." The anger referenced here is not just disagreement or frustration with opposing views but with abusive behavior, defamation, disrespect, and belittlement. There was domestic abuse in Jesus' time as well as our own. And like in our own times, the abusers were often people of high standing who presented themselves as paragons of virtue.

Likewise with the statements about adultery and divorce. I don't think what's being referred to is having desire for a woman. Rather, what's being referred to is finding ways to manipulate a woman and her social circumstances, ingratiating oneself and "alienating her affections," while avoiding a technical sexual violation. So, for example, the Mosaic laws about the husband being required to provide his wife with a certificate of divorce was meant to protect divorced wives, leaving them free to remarry and avoid the opprobrium of adultery. But what frequently happened in practice was that men manipulated this provision so that they could willfully abandon their wives and not provide for them. That is like the technically non-adulterous adultery that Jesus is calling out in the previous verses where the man seeks to improve his position, either financially or sexually, by getting a different wife.

Jesus didn't care if people were "nicer" on the inside. Jesus, like other prophets, wanted people to be treated decently and with respect. Especially those with less social power. Yet, there was something about the way he was so specific in his prescriptions that it came across as radical.

The heart of the Mosaic teachings and the heart of Jesus' gospel are the same—treat all people with basic decency, especially the poor, the widow, and the stranger. But somehow, there are always going to be those who figure out how to profit just a bit more by eliminating the ditch banks, with their habitat for birds and asparagus, efficiently harvesting to the very edge of every field, and justifying to themselves that the gleaners don't really deserve anything.

Which means there is always a need for prophets.

5

A Wedding Feast

And on the third day there was a wedding feast in Cana of Galilee and the mother of Jesus was there. And both Jesus and his disciples were invited to the wedding, And when the wine was exhausted, the mother of Jesus said to him, "They have no wine." And Jesus says to her, "What, madam, is this to me and you? My hour has not yet arrived."

—JOHN 2:14[1]

IN THE GOSPEL OF John, Jesus first appears when he's introduced by John the Baptist: "Behold, the Lamb of God" (John 1:29). The next day, John introduces Jesus to Andrew (the disciple whom Orthodox Christians refer to by the title "the first-called") and another unnamed disciple. Andrew goes out and finds his brother Peter, to whom Jesus immediately assigns the name: "the Rock."

Right away, Jesus' ministry is about relationships, and he seems to be pretty good at them, even without modern day communication tools.

The next day, Jesus decides to go to Galilee. He invites Philip, who was another Galilean from the same town as Peter and Andrew, and Philip goes and finds a friend named Nathanael—who is the one who talks trash about Jesus' hometown with the gibe, "Can anything good come out of Nazareth?"—and famously has a discussion where Jesus calls him "an Israelite

---

1. Hart, *New Testament, A Translation.*

without guile." If you read this without preconceptions about who the original disciples were, what we see here is a high-spirited group of young men, good-humored, perhaps even humorous, getting together and then going for a days-long hike from the Jordan River through the desert up into the hills to Galilee, some eighty to ninety miles away. And on the third day, they show up at this wedding—whether they were invited ahead of time, or they arrived in town and just decided to show up at the celebration isn't clear. But either way, that's a pretty sizable contingent of young men showing up thirsty from their long hike. So, it's not too surprising that the hosts ran out of wine or that Jesus' mom took him aside and pointed out the problem he and his friends were causing. The Gospel of John is known for its misunderstandings, double entendres, and humor.

However, what this passage makes me think of is groups of young men wandering around the various regions of Palestine during the first century. Jesus was not unique or even that unusual in this regard. Josephus, a Jewish historian from that century, mentioned that John the Baptist and his followers (as well as the community that might be the one that wrote the Dead Sea Scrolls), lived out in the wilderness. There are numerous references to "bands of bandits." While among those would be common robbers, it is also clear that groups like the Zealots and the Sicarii were, to one extent or another, religious radicals, political revolutionaries, guerilla soldiers, or some or all of the above. It would be a mistake to think that all of these groups were the same in motivations, rhetoric, or goals, but it would be equally mistaken to use contemporary categories of religious versus secular, political versus social, to describe them.

To understand why there were all these various groups at this historical point, we need some background. Though the Roman Republic had been aggressively expanding around the Mediterranean Sea through war for more than two hundred years before the first intervention in Judea in 63 BCE, the Roman Empire as we understand it today was a relatively new thing during Jesus' lifetime.[2] After Octavian won the civil war that followed

---

2. The Roman Republic is typically dated from 509 to 44 BCE. It was a structured oligarchy in which the leader, or consul, served for a short, defined term, normally a year. It ended when Julius Caesar provoked and won a civil war, was declared dictator in perpetuity, and then was assassinated. The Republic was the government of a city with relationships with other cities, though conquest became the favorite way of gaining and maintaining relationships. The Empire governed the vast territories that had been acquired. By 218 CE, citizenship was extended to the whole empire, not just to citizens of the city. Mary Beard's *SPQR* is an excellent exploration of Rome from its beginning until 218 CE. She begins her story with a crisis in the governance of the Republic in the

A Wedding Feast

the assassination of Julius Caesar in 31 BCE, he consolidated his power and got the Roman Senate to give him the title *princeps* and name him Augustus in 27 BCE. Judea had always been in a precarious position with regard to the military power of its more powerful neighbors. The stories of Israel in Egypt and the exodus led by Moses bespeak the constant awareness of the threat of the power of Egypt to the south. But the northern kingdom of Israel was overcome by the Assyrian Empire in 722 BCE, and then the Babylonian Empire sacked Jerusalem and took many of the leading families of Judea into exile about 145 years later; when they returned, Judea was controlled by the Persian Empire until the Persians were conquered by the Macedonian Alexander the Great in 325 BCE. It was Alexander's Greek successors who ruled both Egypt and the Middle East until the Romans took over in 63 BCE.

There had always been trouble in Jerusalem for whatever kingdom was trying to rule over it. Before the Romans, the Hellenistic empire of the Greeks in Syria had not effectively ruled Judea for over a century. After losing a confrontation with Rome in Egypt, Antiochus IV plundered Jerusalem and disrupted temple worship. The eventual result was the Maccabean Revolt, which led to a Jewish dynasty being established in Jerusalem. The extent of independence of Judea during the Hasmonean dynasty was somewhat ambiguous and varied from one period to another, but the result was that Judeans regarded themselves as an independent people, particularly jealous of the integrity of their religious observances and especially of worship in the temple in Jerusalem.

At the same time that the Romans defeated the Seleucid Empire, they intervened in a civil war between two factions of the Hasmonean dynasty. After that, the Romans were the dominant military force in the area, though things got a bit messy during the civil war that brought Julius Caesar to power, as well as the civil war that followed his assassination in 44 BCE.[3]

To complicate matters further, Herod the Great, though he was the son of a man who had risen to power in the Hasmonean government, wasn't himself from that dynasty. His family was Idumean, and they had only recently converted to Judaism. (Herod the Great should not be confused with

---

early first century BCE.

3. The Romans and the Seleucid Greeks weren't the only powers in the region. The Parthian Empire had displaced the Seleucid Greeks in Iran a century before. They took advantage of the chaos of the Roman civil war to exert influence in Jerusalem, which I describe further on in this chapter. Who was seeking to kill whom and who were allies shifted constantly. Herod's talent was keeping on top of that.

his son, Herod Antipas, who had John the Baptist killed and was in power when Jesus was crucified—the father was a far more competent administrator than his son.)

Herod the Great was a consummate bureaucrat, not lacking in the warrior department either, and so was made governor of Galilee by the Romans. He took advantage of a dispute between claimants of the throne of Judea to get Roman support for him to besiege and take Jerusalem, and the Roman Senate named him King of Judea. During the Roman civil war, he switched sides and convinced the winner, Octavian, that he would be the most competent and loyal client ruler that he could find for Judea before Octavian became the first Roman emperor and named himself Augustus. Thus, Herod and his family were committed Roman clients, and Herod was a supporter of the Roman Empire even before the Empire was formally set up.

As I said, the Roman Empire was a relatively new thing when Jesus was born, and Herod the Great was one of its most competent and dedicated agents. He ruled over an area that included much more than Judea itself, slightly bigger than the current state of Israel and the West Bank. The Jewish people of this area regarded their heritage as Maccabean and Judean, which is to say from the independent kingdoms descended from David and restored in the Maccabean revolt, and not as that of subject peoples of the Babylonian, Persian, or Greek emperors. This made Herod's position as a client of the Roman emperor highly suspect. Herod was clearly not descended from King David, and having God's Anointed[4] being of the house and lineage of David became increasingly important in the popular imagination. Herod was competent at getting major public works built, just as he was also particularly competent at ruthlessly disposing of those he regarded as a threat. Most historians don't find any evidence that the Slaughter of the Innocents as recounted in Matthew 2:16–18 actually happened, but the story probably reflects how Herod was regarded by his subjects.

Apart from the machinations of emperors, kings, and governors, there was also a lot of concern for the proper worship of God and what it was for the Jewish people to be the people of God. The defining place of worship was the temple in Jerusalem. The primary scriptures, the Torah, or five books of Moses, contained the rules for the temple cult and its rationale for existence. The Psalms are hymns which often refer to the

---

4. Anointed could be a simple synonym for king, but the word was *mashiach* and is the origin of messianic speculation and expectation in Judaism. Herod's interest was in political power, but messianism grew during his reign, which was among his problems.

Jerusalem temple and aspects of its worship. For those at a distance from Jerusalem, especially those in the diaspora in what is now Iraq or in Egypt, applying these laws and worshiping the God of Israel separate from the temple required new solutions. That is how the local synagogue came into being—as a place of worship for those far-flung communities who weren't in Jerusalem. What's more, those Jewish diaspora communities didn't keep to themselves; they interacted with the societies around them. We have the writings of philosophers, like Philo of Alexandria, who wrote from a Jewish perspective, explaining and defending Judaism using both the Greek language and Greek philosophical categories.

The "apocrypha" or "deuterocanonical" books, as they're known in Christian Bibles, were all written in the Jewish community at that time. Most were written in Greek, but some were in Hebrew or Aramaic. These reflected many different perspectives, genres, and trajectories in response to the situations that the Jewish people found themselves in during this era, mostly in the diaspora. The community that produced and kept the library called the Dead Sea Scrolls wrote mostly in Hebrew. The texts that aren't copies of biblical books reflect concerns about Jerusalem and Judea, including controversies about the temple, priesthood, and purity.

There were several clearly identifiable groups in Judea in the first century. The Sadducees were identified with the Jerusalem temple and the priesthood. For them, maintaining proper worship of God in the temple was the essence of being God's people. They were, therefore, both extremely conservative and quite willing to accommodate Herod and the Romans for the sake of the safety of the temple. The Pharisees were associated with congregations in the local synagogues and were concerned with applying Jewish scripture to the ways that Jews lived their lives. There was a good bit of variety among them—many scholars argue that Jesus himself was a Pharisee. The Four Gospels are a major source of first-century description of the Pharisees, but each of them was written thirty to sixty years after Jesus, and much of the account of the Pharisees in them reflects the circumstances in which the Gospel was written and reflects their narrative strategy for their own audience. For instance, both Matthew and Luke were written after the destruction of the temple in 70 CE. Matthew was likely writing in Syria or Palestine, where interaction with synagogues and Pharisees was quite common but also fraught with controversy and competition, as both the synagogues and Christian communities struggled to come to terms with how to be religious after the Jerusalem temple, the most essential element of Jewish religion, had been destroyed. In contrast, Luke was probably written substantially later, in a gentile community where he may have had little actual contact with them. Thus, what we read in the New Testament reflects Christian perspectives on the group, which became the most important interpreters of Judaism and its teaching in the period after the Romans destroyed the temple, and thus are not entirely neutral records of the relationship of Jesus and the Pharisees.

The Pharisees were concerned with maintaining Jews as the distinctive people of God through special and separate observance of dietary laws and ritual purity—thus keeping distance from the culture of non-Jewish neighbors. To some extent, this distinctiveness and separation was characteristic of all Jews throughout Judea and the diaspora, but the Pharisees were particularly conscious and devoted to it, while a wide variety of practice characterized different groups of Jews throughout the Mediterranean region. Some would seek Hellenistic education and acceptance in Greek and Roman social and business circles, including participation in athletic events. Even the question of honoring civic deities, indirectly or even directly, was tolerated by some Jewish groups. And of course, across the whole spectrum of Jewish people in Palestine, there were different combinations of commitment and allegiance—these groups did not have hard boundaries.

Other groups that have been identified from that time were: the Zealots, who were particularly concerned with resisting the Hellenistic and Roman occupiers, often violently; the community that gathered the Dead Sea Scrolls (which may or may not be identical with the Essenes), who appear to have dissented from the Sadducean settlement of worship at the temple while they still continued to be occupied with the purity of temple worship and priesthood; and John the Baptist and his followers, who were preaching repentance out in the desert and baptizing at the Jordan River. These parties overlapped in complex ways and interacted with one another, sometimes working together and sometimes in harsh disagreement with one another. What's clear from the New Testament is that Jesus and his followers had contact with all these groups in one way or another.

The Samaritans were separate from all of these groups. There's still a very small Samaritan community in Israel today. They worship the God of Israel and still perform sacrifices according to the precepts of the Torah on Mount Gerizim. Their self-understanding is that they are the authentic descendants of Israel and worship where God decreed, while the Jerusalem temple was a corruption. The Jews in ancient times returned the compliment. They regarded the Samaritans as idolaters and as people who intermarried with pagans. Though it's hard to be sure, the Samaritans were probably descended from Israelites who remained after the Assyrians conquered the northern kingdom of Israel in 722 BCE. Most of our Old Testament reflects the perspective of the southern kingdom of Judah and, in particular, its perspective after the return from the exile in Babylon. The five books of the Torah do not mention Jerusalem, so the Samaritan assertions about their own worship and history are not incredible, at least in terms of anything we can know about history that ancient.

What we do have some reasonable surmise about from the historical record is that during the Second Temple period, the Samaritans constructed a temple on the top of Mount Gerizim. It was destroyed by the army of John Hyrcanus, the Hasmonean king of Judah, in about 110 BCE. This cemented the enmity between the Samaritans and Jews. So, though there was a very substantial population of Samaritans living in regions overlapping with a large number of Jewish towns and they shared the same scriptures, worshiping God with very similar sacrifices, there was little contact and no trust between the two populations.

After Herod's death, his son Archelaus was not able to control Judea, and a revolt, or resistance to Roman taxation, broke out. (Josephus, the Jewish historian, regards this as the beginning of the Zealots and thus the source of the Jewish Revolt in 66 CE that led to the destruction of the temple).[5] This led Augustus to remove Archelaus and institute direct Roman rule. Thus, in a very real sense, the Roman Empire had come to Judea during Jesus' lifetime.

That's a brief orientation to what's going on in first-century Judea when Jesus and his new band of disciples show up at that wedding in the town of Cana in the Galilean region, proceed to make merry, and drink the bride and groom and their family out of the wine so carefully put aside for their guests.

The *1979 Book of Common Prayer* describes this same wedding scene: "Our Lord Jesus Christ adorned this manner of life by his presence and first miracle at a wedding in Cana of Galilee."[6] Hardly the rowdy scene I've been sketching out against the backdrop of a society going through tumultuous changes.

---

5. Josephus, *Flavius Josephus*.
6. *1979 Book*, 423.

It was a troubled time, but how you thought it was troubled depended on what was important to you and the culture you were raised in. The Romans clearly had a part in destabilizing the country, though it was certainly not static before the Romans came in. For Jews, Scriptures were in many ways the most stable touchpoint. The Torah was regarded as being set down by Moses before Israel even entered Judea. It set out the proper worship in the temple—and for many, that worship was the key—either to preserve its status quo or to be outraged at its profanation by those who hadn't kept up with the current way of doing things. The books of the prophets, including the historical books of Samuel and Kings, were an idealized presentation of how Israel and Judah should be governed according to the model of King David and his son Solomon. Those most upset about the political situation viewed this idyllic Davidic kingdom as having been disrupted and blamed the Romans, or Herod, the non-Davidic king, or even the Hasmonean descendants of the Maccabees that preceded Herod.

In this troubled time, people sought solutions, but, for obvious reasons, most didn't try demonstrating in front of the well-equipped Roman garrisons. Usually, the solutions had different admixtures of concern for worship, governance, or of God's miraculous in-breaking into historical events, but it's important to understand that all were religious, spiritual, national, and political at the same time in ways that it would be hard for us to understand today.

It is not surprising that this made the Romans nervous. They were on edge anyway and someone bringing a population together with better health, morale, and social cohesion was a likely threat to a regime that ruled primarily through intimidation and division. Which is why the Gospel of John likely starts off with the miracle at the wedding at Cana, unabashedly using those scenes for symbolic and explicitly theological purposes.

The wedding feast is a widely-used symbol of God's final joyful culmination of this world and its evils, and it is the beginning of Jesus' ministry. "Jesus did this, the first of his signs, at Cana of Galilee, and revealed his glory; and his disciples believed in him" (John 2:11).

The heavy load of symbols may tempt one to think of this as all "theological" or "in the spiritual realm." The symbols abound in all of the Gospels, and Jesus himself likely used such symbols, like the kingdom of God and the Son of Man, in his teaching. But what is essential in all the Gospels, even the Gospel of John with its highly symbolic language and discourses, is that Jesus and his disciples were real people healing real people in the

A Wedding Feast

flesh. They were out there in Galilee touching people, healing them, being human with them, and integrating their broken communities.

> And the Word became flesh and lived among us, and we have seen his glory, the glory as of a father's only son, full of grace and truth. (John testified to him and cried out, "This was he of whom I said, 'He who comes after me ranks ahead of me because he was before me.'") From his fullness we have all received, grace upon grace. (John 1:14–16)

Jesus and his friends spent the largest part of his ministry going from place to place in his home region of Galilee, proclaiming the kingdom of God. That kingdom consisted of the presence of God in joy—bringing people together and healing them. The crowds depicted in the Gospels are motivated and gathered by hope. They bring the sick to Jesus for healing, but that is not just some personal transaction, it's an action of hope—hope that life can be good; life can be abundant. The anxiety and fear of that time gave way to a reality of a compassionate world where there is enough: enough healing, enough bread, the expulsion of demons, and celebration with plenty of wine—wine that just got better as the party went on.

6

Jesus the Healer

Jesus Lamb of God: Have mercy on us.
—Fraction Anthem, *The Hymnal 1982*, S-134

Jesus was primarily a healer. By a quick count, the first eight chapters of the Gospel of Mark have twelve separate accounts of healings—some mentioning Jesus healing large numbers of people. This leaves out exorcisms of demons—a related issue but one I'll consider later. Even though, in the popular mind, Jesus is viewed as general-purpose miracle worker, that's not the case at all.[1]

Nor should Jesus' healings be compared to the kind of healing performed by modern-day medicine. In medical science, the body is a system that has to maintain itself. Medical interventions address problems that are threatening to overwhelm or distort that system, but they only support the

---

1. Aside from healings and exorcisms, the miracles portrayed in the Gospels include: the multiplication of food (and wine) for the crowds, which I'll discuss below; the Transfiguration, which seems to me to be the placing of a Resurrection appearance in the center of at least Mark's Gospel; the stilling of the storm; and the walking on the water. These last two appear in surreal nighttime scenes that convey Jesus' healing presence, calm the terror of the disciples, and the last of which very much resembles Resurrection appearances. Only the miraculous catches of fish (Luke 5:4–11; John 21:5–12), the coin found in the mouth of the fish (Matt 17:24–27), and the cursing of the fig tree (Matt 21:18–22; Mark 11:11–14) are wonders not directly connected with healing or the Resurrection, each carefully placed in the narratives to help Jesus make a point to his disciples.

body in its healing of itself. Even if it looks like the doctor is doing the whole job, like removing a tumor or doing surgery to put a broken bone back together, if the body itself does not respond by healing and adapting to the changes, the patient won't heal and may even die. "The placebo effect" is often mentioned in a way that dismisses healing outside of conventional medical treatment. But the entire point of placebos is to see whether drugs or other treatments have any effect at all. The ways in which the body heals itself are so pervasive that medical researchers cannot tell whether a medicine has any real effect without being very thorough in screening out other ways that healing might occur. There are many ways that a person's body may be encouraged to heal itself, and these are by no means trivial.

As a priest, I have prayed with people for healing. The results often have been subtle or undetectable—the patient or their family taking comfort, perhaps sleeping a little better, and eventually recovering. Sometimes, people die. Actually, all of us die eventually, but some people I've prayed for haven't died yet. And there have been occasions when prayer and anointing have marked the reversal of decline and the beginning of recovery from intense illnesses. The network of love—people praying to God, God loving the person, hands laid on the person, perhaps anointing with oil—that network makes a difference; it affects the healing of a person. A body responds to love, and hope helps a person to thrive. This is not like the "faith healers" you see on TV. Those flashy "miracles" and sudden healings are less about supporting the health of the people who are "healed" than they are about power. There's often a lot of power rhetoric on those shows and its power that those "healers" want for themselves. They make "faith healing" a counterpart to the contemporary misunderstanding of medicine, in which a pill will make you well and the heroic procedure will save you.[2] Appropriate medicine and appropriate prayer assist a person in becoming or remaining healthy.

Jesus was not about having power. He was a healer who loved people, understood them, cared for them, and touched them, and they became healthy. There's no doubt in my mind that Jesus was an extraordinary healer—that he was widely noted as being far more effective than others in

---

2. A person I know well became involved for a short time with a church where this sort of "faith healing" was a major feature. He was asked to be an assistant to the preacher, who would pray for the healing of the person and touch them, after which they would be "slain in the spirit" and fall down in a faint. The assistants were instructed to plant a foot behind the sick person's feet, so that if they didn't spontaneously swoon, they would be tripped backward when pushed by the pastor to be caught by the assistants so they wouldn't hit the floor too hard.

making people well, even casting out frightening and mysterious demons that appeared among people.

I don't want to underplay this or reduce it to our current understanding of how things work. But it is important to remember that the New Testament is comprised of ancient texts that share a literary practice with other ancient texts. Exaggeration, telescoping of time frames, and writing as direct quotations speeches that never happened but bring together what the writer considered to be important about what the speaker had done or taught were characteristic of all ancient texts. This applies not just to poetry, accounts of the gods, or fiction but to histories and even what we would describe as scientific or philosophical writing.

The stories of Jesus healing people don't usually show the process of the body healing or the amount of time Jesus spent with a person. Jesus touches someone and they just get up—already healed. It's a mistake to take this as a magic show and display of power like so-called "faith healers." The Gospel writers who describe these immediate healings also describe Jesus interacting in private and even secretly with people he heals, feeling compassion, telling them of God's mercy, instructing lepers to follow up with the priests, and sometimes defending people who had been healed against people who found it objectionable that a person they'd condescended to as a cripple or beggar was now healthy and acting as their peer.

Healing is a social process as much as it is a physical process. Jesus went around his home country of Galilee healing. Clearly a big part of this is addressing illnesses of individuals that we moderns are inclined to call medical conditions. But the entire society needed healing—Judea and Galilee had been overrun with wars, invasions, and internal dissension, and, just recently, the Romans had asserted direct rule in Jerusalem, settling garrisons of troops in most major towns. It affected all levels of society, undermining morale and social cohesion. Even the hostile response to Jesus' healings may reflect increased hostility and distrust among people. Physical and social illness are intertwined in many ways, and so are their healing. In Mark, right after a large set of dramatic healings, Jesus calls Levi the tax collector to be his disciple and goes to eat at his house along with a bunch of other tax collectors and identified sinners (2:14–17). There's no indication that Jesus was haranguing them to give up their jobs or otherwise change their moral state, but just that he was there to eat and drink beside them, sharing the human condition. And when he was challenged for having fellowship with sinners, his response was, "Those who are well have no need for a physician, but those who are sick" (Matt 9:12). Jesus' outreach to sinners was of a piece with the whole of his healing ministry.

Much of the Gospels, especially the early parts of Matthew, Mark, and Luke, show Jesus wandering around and healing. But in each of these narratives, Jesus sends out groups of his disciples, usually in pairs. Their instructions are to go and find a household and stay with them. It's a lot less like canvassing or drumming up customers and more like dwelling with people and sharing humanity with them. The results are not described in terms of acquiring adherents or people who agreed with their teacher's teachings, rather, "So they went out and proclaimed that all should repent. They cast out many demons, and anointed with oil many who were sick and cured them" (Mark 6:12–13). This is what Jesus and his disciples were up to when they went wandering around Galilee.

In Mark, when the disciples return, Jesus takes them to a deserted place for their own rest and recovery. However, the crowd outsmarts them and is waiting for them there: "And as he went ashore, he saw a great crowd; and he had compassion for them because they were like sheep without a shepherd" (Mark 6:34). After Jesus teaches, he tells the disciples to feed the gathered crowd. Then follows the multiplication of the five loaves and two fish to feed five thousand people. While Jesus' teaching or healing people is mentioned, the story is about Jesus having compassion for this large group that was "like sheep without a shepherd," which is to say confused, lacking direction or coherence, or vulnerable. This feeding is a social demonstration of healing; the people are divided into groups to sit with one another and the limited food is distributed so that everyone has enough. Important as the physical nourishment is, this isn't the establishment of a nutrition supplement program; the people are hungry now, but they're not described as destitute or starving. More than anything, this is a healing of social dissension, manifesting in exaggerated enthusiasm deriving from desperation and anxiety—it's building of community from the ground up. The people eat together, they are nourished, and they are loved. Jesus' mission of proclamation the kingdom of God is more than anything a broad mission of healing.

As I mentioned in the last chapter, the Romans were on edge. This sort of mass assembly would make them suspicious. Someone bringing better health, morale, and social cohesion to a group would be perceived as a threat to a regime that ruled through intimidation and division.

It's clear in the New Testament that John the Baptist was regarded as, in some way, a predecessor to Jesus. He was an earlier contemporary and what he did was regarded as compatible with Jesus' ministry. The Gospel of Luke presents his preaching this way:

> And the crowds asked him, "What then should we do?" In reply he said to them, "Whoever has two coats must share with anyone who has none; and whoever has food must do likewise." Even tax-collectors came to be baptized, and they asked him, "Teacher, what should we do?" He said to them, "Collect no more than the amount prescribed for you." Soldiers also asked him, "And we, what should we do?" He said to them, "Do not extort money from anyone by threats or false accusation, and be satisfied with your wages." (Luke 3:10–14)

Now, the striking thing about John the Baptist's teachings here is that they are simply the baseline of what a decent person is expected to do under either Jewish or Roman law. Sharing clothing and food with those who have none is a very basic obligation, at least within familiar communities where everyone knew one another. It's only when people become strangers that the mutual obligation collapses.[3] Jews were brothers and sisters to one another, not strangers in the law. Likewise, what John had to say to the tax collectors and soldiers was merely what Roman law prescribed for them. At the same time, John's preaching was radical because, as everyone knew, people neglected their obligations to their brothers and sisters, soldiers extorted and bullied people, and tax collectors became wealthy by squeezing extra assessments from the people who had to pay taxes. And what John was especially wrathful about was how ordinary people simply shrugged their shoulders and joined in the culture of corruption.

> You brood of vipers! Who told you to flee the wrath to come? Bear fruits worthy of repentance. Do not begin to say to yourselves, "We have Abraham as our ancestor"; for I tell you, God is able from these stones to raise up children to Abraham. (Matt 3:79)

Repentance for John was not about the forms of religious allegiance or identity, but in restoring the behavioral fabric of the society of Judea.

---

3. See Graeber, *Debt*, 51: "What all such cases of trade through barter have in common is that they are meetings with strangers who will, likely as not, never meet again." In chapter 5 of *Debt* on page 131: "A brief treatise on the moral grounds of economic relations," Graeber explains, "There are three main moral principles on which economic relations can be founded, all of which occur in any human society, and which I will call communism, hierarchy, and exchange."

John the Baptist wasn't opposed to temple sacrifices or individual observance of detailed aspects of the law as the Pharisees taught, but he was very much against anyone choosing to abandon the elements of communal justice and well-being and compromise with the corrupt, unjust rule to make it easy to maintain the status quo of the temple or synagogue.[4]

John was imprisoned by Herod Antipas, the Tetrarch of Galilee, for his criticism of Herod's marriage to his half-brother's ex-wife. People's interpretation of this criticism always says more about them than it does about the situation. Was John puritanical and upset about incest and marital irregularity? Was he upset about corruption, betrayal, and cynical manipulation of family relationships to hold on to power? Was he critical of the Herodian dynasty and Antipas in particular selling out the people of Judea to be clients of the Roman occupiers? Well, we don't have transcripts of any of his sermons, but it would appear to me that all of those things seem to be present. However, the way each of those questions is framed reflects the interests and perspectives of much later times. John was interpreting Scripture and the situation that he saw and was living in. John resembles more than anything the earlier prophets of Israel, such as Jeremiah.

When John was arrested, Jesus began to proclaim repentance and the kingdom of God in Galilee.[5] Basically, he's wandering around the countryside with his crew. There are two interlocking aspects of what Jesus is doing: his teaching about the kingdom of God and his healing and casting out of demons. This is distinct from what we hear of John. Healing is not included in the description of the Baptizer. The most concise description of this is in the Gospel of Matthew, when the followers of John come to Jesus to ask him whether he is the one to come:

---

4. The sources for John the Baptist are pretty limited—basically a passage or two in the writings of Josephus, a Jewish historian writing in the last quarter of the first century, and the Four Gospels. It is a bit difficult to tell how much John's teaching has been elided to Christian teaching in the Gospel presentations. The similarity between John's criticism of the Pharisees and Sadducees and Jesus' controversy with them might stem from that. But it seems clear that the Christians did not have a negative relationship with John or his followers and that John was imprisoned and executed by Herod Antipas for criticizing his marriage and overall morality.

5. The Four Gospels all attest that John the Baptist preceded Jesus in his proclamation of repentance and that Jesus' own ministry started only after his contact with John. Mark (followed by Matthew and Luke) says that Jesus started proclaiming the kingdom of God only after John was arrested. The Gospel of John has them proclaiming and baptizing at the same time.

> Go and tell John what you hear and see: the blind receive their sight, the lame walk, the lepers are cleansed, the deaf hear, the dead are raised, and the poor have good news brought to them. (Matt 11:4-5)

Healing comes first, even in Matthew, the Gospel that emphasizes Jesus' teaching the most of all the four. Jesus and the disciples were out healing and casting out demons. I'll devote another chapter to demons and casting them out, but the good news to the poor entails healing more than anything else. In our modern, middle-class American world, we usually get the wrong idea of who the poor are. In the ancient world, they weren't a small minority of benighted individuals to be pitied and condescended to. The poor were the bulk of the population, struggling to get by in a world where a tiny minority had the wealth and power to take what they want. There were relatively few who were prosperous but not rich. Good news for the poor was good news for all the people.

I rather like to think that the account in the Gospel of Mark is closest to a direct account of how Jesus' ministry developed and looked at the time: healings interspersed with teaching at synagogues, casting out demons, visiting people, and telling them about God's mercy, with controversy building over the ways in which he extended that mercy to people who were perceived not to deserve it—"tax gatherers and sinners"—and his approach to Sabbath observance that was more for refreshment and healing than attention to strictures on behavior. Like John, he called for repentance, and in some ways the behavior change he called for was very similar to John: living decently, compassionately, within the ordinary expectations of the rules and social norms—but also radical in renouncing self-interested manipulations of rules and exploitation of one another.

Jesus announced the kingdom of God. "Repent, for it's at hand!"[6] Perhaps the best way to understand what that phrase meant is by looking at the prayer Jesus taught his disciples. The shortest version (and likely closest to the original) is in the Gospel of Luke:

> Father, hallowed be your name.
> Your kingdom come.
> Give us each day our daily bread.
> And forgive us our sins,
> for we ourselves forgive everyone indebted to us.
> And do not bring us to the time of trial. (Luke 11:2-4)

---

6. Matt 4:17; Mark 1:15.

Jesus the Healer

In praying for the coming of God's kingdom, the disciples have only three things they're asking for: first, daily bread; second, forgiveness of their sins at the same time they forgive their own debtors; third, to be saved from the time of trial (not be brought to the test is another way of translating the same words). This last petition is the most exotic-seeming to modern people—is it a particular aspect of the final judgment and the end of the world? Does it refer to something particular in the history of the early church? Is it any old temptation?

The context of the last part of this prayer is that Jesus and the disciples were walking around Galilee during the early years of direct Roman rule in Judea. People could arbitrarily be seized and punished according to the whim of whoever was in charge locally. There was little practical recourse even against bullying by individual soldiers. One could be dragged before a Roman magistrate and put to the test at any time. It's not so much that people were persecuted for being Christians as they were persecuted for being. As much as for daily sustenance, Jesus' early followers prayed for basic dignity and personal integrity in a world where people were in constant danger of losing them. This is not to say that the image of the trial (temptation/test) was not understood in eschatological or apocalyptic terms. The anticipation of a cosmic crisis with demonic forces causing great suffering and God breaking in for the ultimate, final resolution of this world was widespread in Second Temple Judaism, particularly among those who would come to be known as Christians. But though apocalyptic rhetoric dramatically portrays the discontinuity between this world and the next, it is really born of continuity between the experience of current trauma and crisis, the anticipation of its intensification in mythical proportions, and the hoped-for resolution by God stepping in. Jesus taught this prayer to his disciples, but ultimately it was he who came to the trial: his crucifixion. That crucifixion and Jesus' resurrection were the apocalyptic events for his disciples—God had resolved his trial by raising him from the dead—Jesus had undergone the trial for their salvation.

But in Galilee, this prayer was not referring to Jesus' crucifixion but to life in the kingdom of God. Anticipating the coming of the kingdom and God's will by living quite simply: adequate meals, personal security and integrity, and mutual forgiveness, not just of offenses or crimes against one another, but of debts and other coercive obligations. This is less a program of idyllic, agrarian anarchism than expectation of God to step in and heal a severely broken system.

How Do You Baptize a Whale?

And this takes us back to where we began the previous chapter: the wedding at Cana of Galilee. At the end of the first chapter and beginning of the second chapter of John, Jesus is shown as already having accomplished this task. The story starts with a conversation between Jesus and Nathanael, who, up until that point, has been among the disciples of John the Baptist. Jesus tells him that he saw him "under the fig tree," which may refer to Zechariah 3:10, "On that day, says the Lord of hosts, you shall invite each other to come under your vine and fig tree." That came to be understood as an eschatological, even messianic, prophecy portraying the people of Israel living at peace, prosperity, and security on their own land.[7]

So, Jesus has this conversation with Nathanael (who the last chapter of John refers to as Nathanael of Cana in Galilee), and right after he tells him he will see the angels of God ascending and descending on the Son of Man, the next words are, "And on the third day there was a wedding feast in Cana of Galilee," *and*, "both Jesus and his disciples were invited" (John 2:1-2). I'm pretty sure that the multiplication of the wine in chapter 2 and the multiplication of the loaves in chapter 6 both point to Jesus accomplishing this social healing (and projecting it into the eschatological or ultimate state) in his person and ministry.

Jesus' teaching and his work as a healer are part of the same package. If anything, the teaching is subordinate to the healing and not the other way around. Healing of persons, of families, of marginalized or morally damaged groups, and of rifts caused by the trauma of Roman military intervention all were Jesus' primary ministry in Galilee. Jesus saw Nathanael of Cana in Galilee under the fig tree and led him back to his hometown where the fruit of the vine was provided in superabundance. A wedding feast is a sign and celebration of a healthy and happy society. As the Gospel of John puts it, "Jesus did this, the first of his signs, in Cana of Galilee, and revealed his glory; and his disciples believed in him" (John 2:11).

---

7. There are many indications that John the Baptist's followers formed a group with distinctive beliefs, but no one now knows precisely what those beliefs were, since virtually all the reports of John teaching are in the Gospels, which are at pains to show John's similarity to Jesus. Luke does tell us that John's father was named Zechariah, and this story could be similar to later stories in the Gospel of John, like Nicodemus and the Samaritan woman at the well, where a person from another group comes to Jesus, argues with him in a way characteristic of that group, and then comes to see that Jesus is the Messiah.

7

Casting Out Demons

They went to Capernaum; and when the sabbath came, he entered the synagogue and taught. They were astounded at his teaching, for he taught them as one having authority, and not as the scribes. Just then there was in their synagogue a man with an unclean spirit, and he cried out, "What have you to do with us, Jesus of Nazareth? Have you come to destroy us? I know who you are, the Holy One of God." But Jesus rebuked him, saying, "Be silent, and come out of him!" And the unclean spirit, throwing him into convulsions and crying with a loud voice, came out of him. They were all amazed, and they kept on asking one another, "What is this? A new teaching—with authority! He commands even the unclean spirits, and they obey him." At once his fame began to spread throughout the surrounding region of Galilee.

Mark 1:21–28

"What have you to do with us, Jesus of Nazareth? Have you come to destroy us?" (Mark 1:24). At the very beginning of the action in the Gospel of Mark, when Jesus is first shown teaching, he is confronted by a demon right in the middle of a synagogue service. And it's not just a one-time occurrence: demons, or "unclean spirits," appear constantly throughout the first half of Mark.

In this passage, we see the unclean spirit disrupting Jesus as he teaches—the congregation had been in rapt attention, deeply impressed because Jesus was different, teaching with authority. He was a different kind of teacher, seemingly the master of the Scripture, conveying its news freely and authoritatively.

Jesus is teaching: "The time is fulfilled, and the kingdom of God has come near; repent, and believe in the good news." What that means, essentially, is that Jesus is announcing the kingdom of God. And what is the demon's response? "What have you to do with us? Have you come to destroy us?"[1] Though this demon recognizes Jesus as the Holy One of God, it also perceives the impending kingdom of God as destruction, not life. Notice the use of the plural: "destroy us." The text describes a man with one spirit, but that "us" probably refers to the congregation as a whole.

These demons, or unclean spirits, are always associated with people. Our impression is often that it's one person and one person's demons. But that's not how the Bible uses demonology. Demons occur in communities, families, and societies, even though people may perceive their manifestation in individuals. The synagogue at Capernaum was in a town that was a center of Roman military occupation in a highly anxious time. The Gospels treat the presence of the Romans, particularly their military—soldiers and centurions—as a familiar part of the everyday life in Galilee and Judea. The Jewish historian Josephus discusses a group of Jews, he calls them the Zealots, who thought the Romans were the entire problem and that driving them out was the solution. That's not how any of the Gospels present Jesus, and I don't think it is because the authors were trying to hide who Jesus was.[2] It wasn't that the Romans were not a source of fear and anxiety, but Jesus preached to communities and the individuals that comprised them in their fullness. He respected the agency of the people and their ability to be

---

1. There have been times at parish meetings in troubled congregations where I've experienced something like this.

2. There's every reason to believe that Mark was written before the Jewish Revolt that culminated in the Roman destruction of the temple in 70 CE. The Zealots, including Josephus, were the dominant faction in that revolt, and they persisted and had later success (albeit short-lived) in the Bar Kokhba rebellion half a century later. Paul himself attests that in the 30s CE, he was a member of a Jewish faction (the Pharisees) that were violently opposed to the assembly of Jesus followers—and none of that controversy had anything to do with opposing the Romans, at least not as a military force. Jesus and his followers announcing the kingdom of God were taking a very different route for the survival of the people than the Zealots.

healed and live abundant lives and flourish, even in the midst of a highly adverse and anxious situation.

There are many lenses we can use to analyze dysfunctional, at-times bizarre human behavior: medical, psychological, occult, morality, systems theory, political, or anthropological. All of these modes have been used to analyze Jesus and early Christianity, often quite fruitfully. The bigger problem arises when the texts of Scripture are reduced or translated into a simple explanation and the rest of the story is left aside: "What Jesus really means is . . . !" While the world of two thousand years ago was very different from our own—different language, different culture, different history, different technology—I believe the human dynamics and human realities were similar. What the Gospels describe as "demons" have plenty of analogies in our own experience, and rather than reduce what the Gospel of Mark describes to ways that twenty-first-century people describe them, I am going to try to stay as close as I can to the Gospel description. Demons are depicted as intertwined with humans, yet having a distinct existence and some sort of awareness. They are never a benign force (though there may be benign or beneficial spirits in some other contexts).[3]

Among human beings there are many sorts of things that are real. The classical elements: earth, water, air, and fire. The natural world's geology and zoology. My dog is real. My clothes are real. The food I eat to sustain myself is real, though what I eat and drink might not be what others accept as real food because of different places, times, and customs.

Then there are human constructs that we accept as real, like the construct of families. We think we know who our family is, but sometimes we find out it's not quite as it seems. I once had a friend, a young woman who believed she was an only child. But when she was in her late twenties, her father died, and, at his funeral, she discovered she had at least five half-siblings that her father had with that many women other than her mother. It was disconcerting because, for some of those involved, all of this man's descendants were their family while for others, the lack of

---

3. William Stringfellow develops a typology of "principalities and powers" in his book *An Ethic for Christians and Other Aliens in a Strange Land*, pp. 67–94. Besides demons, Stringfellow described an array of powers that are manifest in our world that have lives and exert influence in the world separate from the control that people may believe that they have over them. Some, like the law or corporations, have ambiguous existences, being both good and bad. Their neutrality is only malign insofar as they participate in the fallenness of all creation. This chapter is focusing on demons and the demonic, and my views aren't exactly the same as Stringfellow's.

ongoing relationships or even knowledge of their existence meant that they regarded none of them as family. And America's grievous sin of slavery and racism has meant that people discover they have unknown siblings who were born of terrible and unequal relationships, including rape. That is the case with relatives of mine who found out as adults that they had a Black cousin because their grandfather had a premarital affair with a servant—a child that the white half-siblings supported financially, but didn't publicly acknowledge.

It's not unlike that Facebook relationship status from a few years ago: "it's complicated." Families are complicated. Disavowing a relationship doesn't make a relationship not exist, just as being unaware of it doesn't mean it doesn't exist.

As complicated as families are, powers, principalities, and demons are far more complex. The biggest, most obvious demonic force (at least for twenty-first-century Americans) is racism. A naïve approach to racism is to regard it as a conscious decision by individuals to be bigoted, discriminatory, and hateful for the sake of their own selfish interests. Yet limiting racism to the conscious actions by such individuals completely ignores the experience of anyone who has actually experienced racism. For African Americans, the experience of being demeaned, discriminated against, ignored, devalued, and not taken seriously is pervasive. I am white, but as I became the pastor of a Black church and got to know its people, I was astonished to witness the way that they were often treated by the administration of the wider church. These administrators were all educated white people and almost all would be described as liberal. They were often earnest participants in anti-racism training offered by the diocese at some of its more well-off churches. Yet my parishioners were still ignored and treated with disrespect when they came to the white hierarchy to resolve administrative problems or to ask for their support for projects they wanted to work on to support the people of their very poor neighborhood.

It's wrong to think that these were the worst that New York City or the white Episcopal Church has to offer. They are quite typical people, of the sort that might read this book. We are all part of a system of racism—a system where people of privilege ignore all the ways that their privilege derives from the suffering of others. It's a spiritual force and much more complex than even this implies. Racism is a living demonic power that reproduces itself throughout generations. The social strands of fears and hates and greediness and desire for social respect intertwine, resulting in a demon that has a life of its own. Earnest classes and commitments by individuals don't control it or make it go away. No individual can make themselves "not a racist." Surely, it's possible to see individuals who are possessed by this demon and whole communities totally under its thrall. But this demon crops up suddenly in unexpected places, manifested among people who "thought they were done with all that." More on this later.

In the fifth chapter of Mark, Jesus gets out of the boat on the side of the Sea of Galilee, across from Capernaum and Galilee where he had been teaching, in an area largely populated by gentiles called the Decapolis—the Ten Towns. And he's confronted by a man:

> Immediately a man out of the tombs with an unclean spirit met him. He lived among the tombs; and no one could restrain him anymore, even with a chain; for he had often been restrained with shackles and chains, but the chains he wrenched apart, and the shackles he broke in pieces; and no one had the strength to subdue him. Night and day among the tombs and on the mountains he was always howling and bruising himself with stones. (Mark 5:2–5)

It's a frightening vision—a man with superhuman strength, breaking shackles and chains, angrily approaching Jesus. I am not really sure why he is portrayed as coming "out of the tombs," the dwelling of the dead, but it certainly sets a scene. And the man is certainly tormented, howling, and hitting himself with rocks.

> He ran and bowed down before him; and he shouted at the top of his voice, "What have you to do with me, Jesus, Son of the Most High God? I adjure you by God, do not torment me." (Mark 5:6–7)

Jesus recognized the demon and calmly ordered it to come out of the man. The demon (and the man?) were clearly frightened: "Do not torment me!"

"What is your name?"

"My name is Legion; for we are many" (Mark 5:9).

The demon is many—multi-faceted, fragmented. The man is tortured and self-destructive. A danger to himself and to others—literally disintegrating while he lives among the dead. In this episode, Jesus is entirely compassionate toward him, yet the demon within him, his tormentor, begs Jesus not to torment him. There is a great ambiguity with this demon, and really with all demons: in some ways the demon is identified with the person, their actions, their expressions—is the demon aspects of the person?

The demon is also separate and distinct from the person. Its goals aren't for the good of the person, nor is the demon under the control of him—quite the opposite, a person with an unclean spirit finds themselves under the spirit's control. In this case, the fragmentation is emphasized, the demon is not in a simple linear relationship with the person—it's all over the map. More importantly, perhaps, this demon, this spirit, this dynamic, is not in any way limited to the "infected" person. In this memorable episode, the demons ask Jesus not to send them out of that country and then beg to be sent instead into a nearby herd of pigs. (Joke's on the Legion; the pigs stampede into the lake and drown!)[4]

As the story continues, it is clear that this demon possession affects the entire region and community. The man is now sitting there, freed of the demon, in his right mind. And that frightened the people from the community more than when he had been crazy, breaking chains, and roaring out from the tombs. They begged his healer to leave. Casting out their demons disrupted their lives. They regarded healing as worse than demonic possession—at least in the way it affected them. The man certainly didn't feel welcome there; he begged Jesus to take him along. But Jesus sent him back to that community.[5] He's to share what God did for him and the mercy he's received. There's no implication that he has to confront enemies or the most uncomfortable people, but the text says that he went around that region of the Decapolis proclaiming what Jesus had done. Overall, people were amazed at the healing; the healing had a positive effect on the community, even though the immediate reaction of those closest to the situation was dismay and rejection of both the healer and the healed.

Moderns generally look for discrete causes and unitary explanations for things that go wrong. It's one thing or another—a germ causes a disease, a psychiatric disorder causes erratic behavior, people do bad things because they have bad intentions—*and*—if you have good intentions, then that must mean you aren't doing bad things. The world has never been so

---

4. The prominence of the herd of swine and the swineherd going into the town to tell the people there about this calamity emphasizes that this is a gentile area. The demon possession doesn't impinge simply on people but on farm animals, the environment, and the local economy.

5. Translations differ with regard to whom Jesus sent the man: NRSV and RSV say, "Go home to your friends." David Bentley Hart translates it as, "Go to your house, to your own family." This is because the text in Mark is not specific, rather it uses an adjective meaning "your" without a specified object. Perhaps, "Go to your house and your own," would be kind of literal. These translations are not in any way wrong, but no weight should be put on *who* Jesus is telling the man to tell what God has done.

simple. Demons are Legion. Causes are multifarious. Evil comes from many directions and in many guises. And the shape of any event or interaction involves many forces, and those forces are not just physical, or psychological, or organic, or ideological. The consequences of one good thing in the internal life of an individual can show up in the physical world at a distance, like the swine plunging over the cliff after Jesus healed this man of his demonic possession. There is lots of power in isolating the effects of single factors, in science or in medicine, but in the lived world, multiple factors occur simultaneously, all having their effect on the whole.

In this story, demon possession affects the whole of the social fabric around the man. Indeed, many in the community were more distressed by the disappearance of the demons than by their ongoing, chronic presence in the man, hurting himself up among the tombs. We see this kind of dynamic playing out in our own lives. When one person begins to change self-destructive behavior, their family, church, or place of employment reacts; first by trying to restore the old pattern—keeping them trapped in the dysfunction—and if, despite this, the person succeeds in changing, another person in community with them, who seemed to be fine, will start acting out in destructive or even crazy ways.

Demons are diffuse, crazy, and incoherent. Yet they also have a shape, a focus, and coherence. They take their shape from human beings—a community of some sort—but often manifesting in a specific individual (the "possessed" one); their purpose is chaos and evil, yet that chaotic existence is maintained by themes that make sense to humans. They are themes of resentment, hatred, and distrust, supported by images and narratives from the world they inhabit. Demons often have physical effects and manifestations. Immediately after the Transfiguration in the Gospel of Mark, Jesus encounters a man who says,

> "Teacher, I brought you my son; he has a spirit that makes him unable to speak; and whenever it seizes him, it dashes him down; and he foams and grinds his teeth and becomes rigid." (Mark 9:17–18)

Sometimes, we interpret these biblical descriptions as being physical or mental illnesses for which modern medicine has provided diagnoses. Indeed, the outward symptoms of epilepsy as popularly understood all seem to be there. But it's not simply a matter of misunderstood disease for which we have a modern name and explanation. The treatments that modern medicine might have for similar conditions are entirely beside the point.

How Do You Baptize a Whale?

Jesus has been away and the disciples have been trying to cope on their own.[6] The situation in this family is dire and the disciples have been trying whatever they can to address it to no avail. The whole community is disrupted by the presence of this demon. A big argument is the first thing that's mentioned here: rather than join the argument, Jesus asks the father of the boy to describe the boy's situation in detail.[7] The father asks Jesus for help and compassion, and Jesus reassures him. Jesus' command to the demon isn't showy or flashy, but the departure of the demon puts the boy into another seizure, leaving him unconscious, and many observers feared he was dead. Jesus' answer to his disciples when they ask him why they had no success in casting out the demon was, "This kind can come out only through prayer and fasting," makes me think there was more to the healing process for the boy than the simple words in the text.

It is compassion, prayer, and courage that cast out the demons, not theatrics or violence. Indeed, we could think of demons as the incarnation of hatred and violence, much as Jesus is the incarnation of God's love—compassion, mercy, and affirmation. The demons have to leave when confronted with Jesus' compassion. The demons are forces of nothingness and death—the one thing that is real is compassion.

Demons cause so much real damage, how is it that they are not real? Make no mistake about it: they have a reality. That reality is an amalgam of fear, hatred, nihilistic greed, and despair. Rather than being identifiable as discreet emotions, values, thoughts, or located in individuals, demonic forces mix these things up—often a "possessed" individual is manifesting aspects of some or all of these things, not from within themselves but from their environment.

The most pervasive demonic force for those of us with European and American cultural backgrounds over the past few centuries is racism. Believing that their own culture was the measure of true civilization and that they possessed all truth and virtue, either in the Catholic Church and its sacraments, or for the Protestants in the infallible Bible and their clear

---

6. This is an important turning point in the Gospel which I discuss in some detail in the next chapter. I believe this episode and the entire remainder of chapter 9 of Mark are addressing issues the church faced after Jesus' resurrection, when he was no longer present with the disciples.

7. It's not a good idea to put too much weight on the apparent alacrity with which the demon is dispatched. Telescoping of time and leaving out steps that normally take some time are typical of ancient texts, and this exorcism has more steps and lasts longer than many of Jesus' healings and exorcisms.

understanding of it, Europeans embarked on the conquest of the world—a conquest that included the enslavement and subjugation of a large portion of the world's people. But because their rationale was so founded in the universal and absolute truth of their religious heritage—and that heritage contained many condemnations of enslavement of others, disrespecting others, and gathering excessive wealth—it became necessary to embark on a massive process of denial and rationalization. Avarice, cynicism, exploitation, and callousness were papered over with a virtue labeled as "civilization" and a belief in the essential superiority of the white race (though the concept of a white race itself was made up for this very purpose). Each refusal to see racism for the evil that it is only fuels that giant demon. It infects our society still—or perhaps not still, but in some ways more than ever. One can see obvious irruptions of it in lynchings—or Donald Trump rallies.

But besides these obvious and violent forms of racism, there are other patronizing and condescending forms of racism that characterize many of us who believe that we are "allies" in the struggle. Who is listened to? Who is respected? Are they those that fit the narrative a particular white group wants to hear? We gloss over our disrespect and condescension and don't recognize how it's demonic. We don't recognize this as demonic because it's ingrained. Churches with tens or even hundreds of millions of dollars in endowments might put out a plaque acknowledging that their wealth came from nineteenth century merchants whose shipping interests were primarily founded on the slave trade. Yet when actions are proposed that would assist poor parishes across the river to continue to serve their neighborhoods, they fight tooth and nail to preserve all the corpus of the endowment that comprises that legacy. The demonic force of racism keeps this from even being perceived, let alone acknowledged.

Racism is a white problem that affects non-white people. It's important to white people to regard themselves as virtuous, compassionate, and caring people, which means that their selfishness, condescension, and manipulation adds more to the system of violence and disrespect that Black and Brown people experience daily. I was the priest at a church in the south Bronx for a number of years. It took some time for me to learn how to listen to the church members, but when they began to trust me, I began to hear things that happened to these people of Caribbean heritage—things they were generally quiet about in order to maintain their dignity. Pretty much daily, they would suffer indignities, at times egregious and unambiguously degrading and disrespectful. Unless something came up in a conversation, they wouldn't mention them because, after all, "that's just the way white folks act."

That is the way white people act—and most of the time, it's not something we even notice—never even registering in our own minds our disrespect or condescension. This blindness is why I analyze this as part of a pervasive demon instead of as individual missteps. Good intentioned people who regard themselves as responsible, compassionate, and aware participate in the lacerating actions of racism every day. Genuinely good people—not just the cynical or intentionally nasty.

Demons are pervasive and damage humans terribly. They are the forces of death—encouraging despair, conflict, and humiliation. Demons rush us toward Nothingness[8] and self-harm.

These sound like reinforcing cycles that can't be escaped, and, indeed, we often don't escape them. Racism has been around for a very long time.

Yet how did Jesus approach demons? He was calm, looked on the person with compassion, and addressed the demon directly: "Come out!"[9] Jesus was a human being living from God's point of view. He was perfect compassion and I don't expect my own compassion or anyone else's to be as clear or effective as him in casting out these demons. Yet we do face demonic forces all the time, and the only power that is effective in casting them out is our compassion.

The thing I emphasize the most when preparing people for baptism are the three questions that begin the examination of candidates for baptism (*1979 Book of Common Prayer*, 302):

---

8. The twentieth-century Swiss theologian Karl Barth wrote at length about Nothingness. "The character of Nothingness derives from its ontic peculiarity. It is evil" (Barth, *Church Dogmatics*, 3.3:503). I don't profess to fully understand Barth's meaning in its entirety. God's will is entirely good and Nothingness is that which is outside God's will. Barth's discussion of this includes the implication of this for the Election of humans for salvation and the state of creation, in very long and dense arguments, and his discussion of Nothingness is reputed to be among the most difficult to grasp. However, it can be appreciated that evil is the turning away from goodness and thus God; and that isn't simply some individual decision or individual laziness but something that is cumulative, huge, and can't simply be decided by good intentions. Yet it is truly Nothing—more akin to Death than to anything that exists, and in that it is not like mortality but more like despair. I don't take this from Barth, but I regard demons as the irruption of Nothingness into human life and society.

9. Mark 1:25. See also John 11:43, when Jesus restores Lazarus to life and orders him to come out of the tomb.

- Do you renounce Satan and all the spiritual forces of wickedness that rebel against God?
- Do you renounce the evil powers of this world which corrupt and destroy the creatures of God?
- Do you renounce all sinful desires that draw you from the love of God?

Renunciation of demons is possible in the sense that it is possible to join in the compassion of God and to be aware of the constant assaults of these demons. This doesn't make them disappear in a moment or a lifetime, but it's possible to join with the one who can cast out these demons, to have both humility and courage, to give up fearfulness, and be willing to live in ways where we don't hide behind our privilege. This is often described as self-sacrifice or even heroic, but I don't quite buy that. It's simply living as decent human beings.

Jesus cast out demons and the demons reacted against him. His compassion continued to the end. It's possible to read Jesus' crucifixion as the chief demons of the ancient Mediterranean world—war, empire, and enslavement—focusing on Jesus all the forces of death and nothingness and killing him.

After all, one of the most pervasive descriptions of Jesus' death and resurrection in ancient Christian theology was of his defeat of the demonic forces and liberating all the dead from hell.

8

The Resurrection of Jesus

> If Christ has not been raised, then our proclamation has been in vain and your faith has been in vain. We are even found to be misrepresenting God, because we testified of God that he raised Christ.
>
> —1 Corinthians 15:14–15

God raised Jesus from the dead. The fundamental thing that defined Christianity from its outset was this belief. Jesus, of course, had followers before his crucifixion. He healed, cast out demons, and taught, but it would be meaningless to call the people he interacted with Christians. The community we call church was created through the proclamation of Jesus' death and resurrection—only through that lens does Jesus come into focus. The Gospels, especially the Gospel of Mark, say that outright.

> And as they were coming down out of the mountain he enjoined them that they should not relate the things they saw to anyone, except when the Son of Man should rise from the dead. (Mark 9:9)

Proclaiming and interpreting Jesus' resurrection is the most important thing that a Christian preacher can do. It's the foundation of everything. In our days of skepticism and doubt, when the church finds itself on its back foot for all sorts of reasons, I've seen many colleagues defensively insist on what they regard as a maximalist and undiluted position. Roughly, that means that Jesus rose up out of the tomb in his physical body and was there for anybody to see, feel, and touch. The corollary of these assertions would be that God somehow mended all the damaged organs ravaged by Jesus' time on the cross[1] (except for some reason, not his hands, feet, and side that still bore the stigmata) and that he was continually present walking around with his old friends for forty days.

However, this is not at all what the biblical accounts portray and it doesn't really fit with the apostles' proclamation of Jesus' resurrection. God having raised Jesus from the dead is the essential message, but how do we understand that and why is it of such world-shattering importance?

There are about twenty accounts of the resurrection of Jesus in the New Testament. In some of the most prominent ones, people who knew him in life saw the resurrected Jesus close up, yet they did not recognize him. In Luke, two disciples walking out of Jerusalem toward the village of Emmaus encounter Jesus and talk with him for hours without realizing who he is. After he had explained all the scriptural precedent and logic behind the Messiah being crucified and resurrected, they invited him to stop with them for dinner. It was only when he broke the bread that they recognized him. Then, he disappeared from sight.

In John, Mary Magdalene was the first to visit Jesus' tomb and found it empty. She summoned Peter and the Beloved Disciple who went inside and saw that the tomb was empty and the cloths that wrapped Jesus had been left behind. When they left, Mary Magdalene saw two angels inside the tomb who asked her why she was weeping:

> She said to them, "They have taken away my Lord, and I do not know where they have laid him." (John 20:13)

She's looking into the tomb, addressing the angels in grief and despair. Then,

> When she had said this, she turned around and saw Jesus standing there, but she did not know that it was Jesus. Jesus said to her, "Woman, why are you weeping? For whom are you looking?" Supposing him to be the gardener, she said to him, "Sir, if you have carried him away, tell me where you have laid him, and I will take him away." Jesus said to her, "Mary!" She turned and said to him in Hebrew, "Rabbouni!" (which means Teacher). (John 20:14–16)

She turns around, away from the angels, and looks directly at Jesus. She sees him but does not recognize him. And Jesus talks to her, asking

---

[1]. I won't go into grisly details, but crucifixion was death by torture—nails in hands and feet were the least of the torture and being stabbed with a spear was a mercy.

why she is weeping and whom it is she is looking for. Even after hearing his voice, she still mistakes him for the groundskeeper. She's directly addressing him when he calls her by name. It's very strange, therefore, that the text then says that "she turned." Many interpreters imagine all sorts of contorted choreography to make sense of this, but the most satisfactory explanation I've heard is that this is typical of the Gospel of John's portrayal of a person's enlightenment or conversion—a moment of repentance, i.e., a "turning."[2]

The twenty-first chapter of the Gospel of John is a sort of coda, which some scholars think may have been added after this gospel was completed. In it, Peter and six other disciples are back in Galilee. They decide to go fishing, which turns into a miserable, fruitless night with no catch to be had. Around dawn, they see Jesus walking on the shore. He tells them where to cast their nets and suddenly they have a superabundant haul of fish. They don't recognize Jesus until this happens, and then the Beloved Disciple says, "It is the Lord!" (v. 7). Peter, being Peter, puts on his clothes and jumps in the water to swim over to be with Jesus, who is on the beach cooking fish in the most ordinary, human manner one might expect from a local fisherman.

In each of these stories, Jesus is really there, but people who knew him intimately before he died (and should recognize him immediately) don't know who Jesus is until they see him through the eyes of faith. Likewise with other stories in the Gospels that emphasize Jesus' physical presence. Jesus suddenly appears in the midst of the disciples—even in securely locked rooms. He appears out of nowhere; he demonstrates that he can be touched; in the Gospels of Luke and John, he eats fish. Yet his mere appearance is not enough for true recognition. In Luke 24, after the two who encountered Jesus on the road to Emmaus rush back to tell the disciples, Jesus appears in the midst of them and they initially think he's a ghost.

In Emily Wilson's marvelous translations of the *Iliad* and the *Odyssey*,[3] it's clear that the author of these poems, which were already ancient texts when Jesus appeared on the scene, believed that people who died became shades or ghosts and continued to have an attenuated and sad life in the underworld. Some who died and weren't properly buried didn't make it to the underworld proper and wandered around aimlessly. This was regarded as the worst possible fate—one that Achilles tried to perpetrate on Hector

---

2. I first heard this from Sandra Schneiders, IHM, in her course "The Spirituality of the Gospel of John" at the Jesuit School of Theology in Berkeley in the spring of 1981. The word *strepho*, which is used in this passage, can be understood as a physical turning or as a reorientation or inward change.

3. Homer, *Odyssey*, 11.279–300.

The Resurrection of Jesus

by taking his body, desecrating it, and leaving it out to be eaten by dogs.[4] This wasn't an Israelite or Jewish view of the afterlife, but in the Hellenistic world of the Roman Empire, these views were part of the popular consciousness to one extent or another. So when the disciples were startled and terrified by Jesus' appearance, they thought they were seeing such a spirit. Jesus takes them to task for this and assures them that his existence is in no way attenuated—they can touch and feel him, and he eats with them. Their fearfulness is replaced with faith and they recognize him. The same thing happens during the two appearances to the disciples in the locked room in the Gospel of John. Though the Gospel has just said that Mary Magdalene had told the disciples that Jesus had appeared to her and told her that he was ascending to "my father and your father, to my God and your God" (John 21:17), the disciples locked themselves in their house "for fear of the Jews"[5] as they cowered in their house, Jesus came and stood among them and said, "Peace be with you" (John 21:19). Then Jesus showed them his hands and his side—showing the wounds of his physical body. Only after this does it say that the disciples rejoiced when they saw Jesus. Jesus then breathed on them saying, "Receive the Holy Spirit, those whose sins you forgive are forgiven, those who you hold fast, are held fast"[6] (John 21:22–23). After Jesus has gone, Thomas arrives and is skeptical of their account. When Jesus appears again, showing the same physical signs to Thomas, he responds, "My Lord and my God!" (John 21:28).

---

4. Achilles doesn't succeed, only because the gods intervene on Hector's behalf. Homer, *Iliad*, Books 23–24, 545–610.

5. The author of the Gospel of John, writing at the end of the first century when Christian relations with the Jewish community had become embittered, characterized controversies and danger to Christians as coming from "the Jews" as opposed to the Romans or any sub-group of Judeans. It's nonetheless quite plausible that the disciples were rightly fearful of those who had crucified Jesus, whether, as John says, it was the Jewish mob or of the Roman authorities rooting out Jesus' partners in sedition.

6. Sandra Schneiders examined this passage closely. She traced out every reference to the word meaning "hold fast" (κρατεω [*krateo*]) in every Greek lexicon and found that the definition "retain the sins" of someone, only occurs in those who infer it from this single sentence in John among all of written Greek. The parallel construction in this sentence is better understood as the Holy Spirit enables the disciples to forgive others and to hold those same people close. In the next paragraph, Thomas arrives and has a controversy with them about the resurrection, and they hold him with them until the next week when he encounters Jesus at the same place. The inference that it is giving authority to the apostles to retain people's sins is best understood as reflecting the authoritarian preferences of later church authorities.

How Do You Baptize a Whale?

The emphasis on Jesus' physical presence in these passages is not a crass materialism but rather is used to show that there is nothing attenuated about Jesus' life as resurrected—there's nothing ghostly or merely "spiritual"—rather his life is as full and compelling as ever. It makes no sense to try to harmonize all of these images of the resurrected Jesus because Jesus can't be reduced to a single coherent explanation. Confusion is a big part of the disciples' experience—they often don't recognize him! The variety in the accounts of Jesus' resurrection are unified by the belief that the forces of death have done their worst and had their full effect, but God has raised Jesus to life that is complete and even more full than before. Those forces of death (demons, hatred, exploitation, persecution of the helpless, nihilistic selfishness, hopelessness) have all been refuted in this one life—the life of healing, compassion, generosity, and mercy that Jesus lived in this world.

Was the experience of Jesus' resurrection the same for all these early Christians? It's impossible to say, though it's probably at least true that as all individuals differ, they experience even simultaneous identical phenomena differently. The earliest account of Jesus' resurrection that has any detail is in Paul's first letter to the Corinthians:

> For I handed on to you as of first importance what I in turn had received: that Christ died for our sins in accordance with the scriptures, and that he was buried, and that he was raised on the third day in accordance with the scriptures, and that he appeared to Cephas, then to the twelve. Then he appeared to more than five hundred brothers at one time, most of whom are still alive, though some have died. Then he appeared to James, then to all the apostles. Last of all, as to someone untimely born, he appeared also to me. (1 Cor 15:38)

Elements of this summary appear in the accounts in the Four Gospels, notably the reference to Cephas[7] and the Twelve (which the Gospels pedantically correct to Eleven because Judas Iscariot was excluded), as well as the references to appearances to other disciples. Interesting, at least to me, is that Paul makes no reference to appearances to women[8] despite the

---

7. Cephas is an Aramaic word meaning "rock" and is the equivalent of the Greek πετρος (*petros*), the nickname Jesus gave Peter, whose given name was Simon. Paul's usage of Cephas probably indicates that was what Peter was actually called until Christianity became more thoroughly Greek-speaking.

8. The New Revised Standard Version, in an effort to promote inclusive language, translates αδελφοις (*adelphois*) as "brothers and sisters," but it is the masculine plural, not one that normally includes "sisters," which is a different form of the word.

prominent role that Mary Magdalene and other women play in the resurrection narratives of Mark, Matthew, John, and Luke. This appears to be a formula that Paul inherited and is repeating. It emphasizes the leaders of the church at the time Paul was writing. In adding his own name to this list, he makes no distinction between the appearance of Jesus to the first apostles and to him, though his reported visitation was several years later, and the depiction of the event in the Acts of the Apostles (which was written many years after Paul) seems more like an auditory vision than the physical appearances in the resurrection accounts in Luke and John as well as Matthew. In equating his own encounter with the resurrected Jesus with the resurrection appearances of the tradition (probably about twenty years before he wrote this), Paul does not regard Jesus' resurrection as limited in time or space—even for those first appearances.

Paul does regard the resurrection as bodily. Later in the same chapter, he discusses this at length like so:

> But someone will ask, "How are the dead raised? With what kind of body do they come?" Fool! What you sow does not come to life unless it dies. And as for what you sow, you do not sow the body that is to be, but a bare seed, perhaps of wheat or of some other grain. But God gives it a body as he has chosen, and to each kind of seed its own body. (1 Cor 15:35–38)

Paul emphasizes the reality of the bodily resurrection, both of Jesus and of everyone God chooses to raise at the last day. His concern, similar to Luke, is to emphasize that this resurrected body is in no way attenuated but as fully real as any physical body that anyone has ever had—in fact more real, being glorified by God.[9]

In popular discourse, including many very educated people who haven't developed consistent philosophical theories, there appears to be a default worldview that everything came into being from dead matter, chemicals and suchlike, and that as entropy increases, everything gradually falls back into death. Thus, death is the ultimate reality in our society. I have no dispute with chemical processes or those of physics. But I object to the naïve framing that accords this ultimate privilege to dead matter. We live in a world populated by living beings; as humans, our attention focuses mostly on our species—the things that people do and the things that people make.

---

9. The concerns that Jesus' appearances might be merely a phantom or a ghost were probably something that came up later as Christianity became more widespread and debates with nonbelievers were more established.

Among the things that people do is study the structures and interactions of matter, the details of the physical. But even among the purest of pure scientists, ultimately these things are studied for their significance—their significance to human life. The ability to end life, to reduce living things to dead matter, only seems like ultimate power. But it's not. It is delusion—the forces of death are demonic; they are, more than anything, expressions of fear. Courage and compassion are more real and lasting than any of these death-dealing delusions.

God raised Jesus from the dead and he was more fully alive than we can understand. The Source of our universe is the source of all matter, all life, and all compassion. In the resurrection, Jesus appeared to his disciples and they were confused; they couldn't explain it—their emotions ran the gamut from immense fear to overwhelming joy—and they felt heightened uncertainty alongside absolute faith. Primarily, what the disciples experienced was great joy at the goodness of God and the triumph of life over death. But this joy emerged out of the intensity of the ambiguity of real life and the drama of life arising in the context of the arrayed forces of death. Jesus had lived a life of healing and freedom. He was compassionate with those he encountered and confronted those who hurt the weak or the poor. His stories helped his listeners question their own behavior and expanded their view of others. And he was merciful in the way he lived with others—so merciful that those inclined to sanctimony were outraged. He was so free that those who wanted to oppress others were threatened, especially the agents of the Roman occupiers and those who benefited from being aligned with them. His life was abundant and joyful, and that is what occasioned the demonic and self-serving servants of death to use all the powers of death to kill him. And they did. He died.

He arose from the dead and appeared to those who were confused, to those who were afraid, to those who grieved, and to those who felt defeated. The powers of death did not defeat him, and he brought God's mercy to those assailed by those powers: "Peace be with you."[10] The threats and bullying of those who have power, whether locally, nationally, or globally, are not the final reality. Life, compassion, and respect for God's children—all of God's creatures—is the crucial reality. In Jesus' resurrection, it is *possible* to live that way, in accord with what's critical and leave behind fear, violence, and bullying.[11] Bullies have no way to the truth. Life continues beyond any

---

10. Luke 24:36; John 20:19, 26.

11. There's no doubt that Christians have consistently failed to avail themselves of this

of the ravages wrought by the powerful and callous. Life belongs to the humble and compassionate. It is not that people do not suffer or that people do not die. Compassion and comfort for those who suffer—and at some point, each of us is one of those—is essential to living humanly. It is nihilism and death that disappears, not life and compassion.

The Gospel of Mark is the earliest of the four Gospel accounts. It is closely related to Paul, both chronologically and in its focus, especially in the frequent occurrence of the word *euangelion* (ευαγγελιον). That's the word for gospel, but it's often translated as "good news." It was used in ordinary Greek to signify an announcement, usually one distributed by an official, which would be distributed to make sure people knew of something important—more serious than a press release—usually something good about what the official had done. Both Paul and Mark use it to refer to the proclamation of Jesus, the essential focus of their work. The *euangelion* is the announcement of what *God* has done—he has raised Jesus from the dead! So now it is *the* Announcement: the Gospel. So, in the Revised Standard Version, Mark begins, "The beginning of the Gospel of Jesus Christ" (1:1). Seems like pretty mundane stuff if it's referring to the book of Mark as a story in sixteen chapters. But it's perfectly reasonable to translate the same words as, "The origin of the announcement of Jesus Christ."

Before any other gospels and narratives and collections of teachings were written down, this story as we have it in Mark, beginning with the proclamation of John the Baptist and ending with Jesus' crucifixion and the young man's[12] announcement of the resurrection to the women, was written. For a generation that had been born long after Jesus' ministry and didn't know the context (at least in any definitive way), it's an explanation of the *euangelion*—the proclamation, as Paul put it in 1 Cor 15:3–5,

---

possibility. Fear is ubiquitous and the church often chooses to organize itself around the "smart" ideas of worldly power. Occasionally, I wonder whether the Episcopal Church has a standard of electing bishops who don't believe in the resurrection. Over the centuries Christians have engaged in bullying, wars, pogroms, and sly oppression of the weak. Choosing power over the love of God. By using the name of Jesus to do these things the church blasphemes God and all the children and the oppressed that comprise the Body of Christ. "We have followed too much the devices and desires of our own hearts. We have offended against thy holy laws. We have left undone those things which we ought to have done; And have done those things which we ought not to have done; And there is no health in us" (*Book of Common Prayer 1928*, 6).

12. The other Gospels make it clear that an angel spoke to the women, but Mark says "a young man dressed in a white robe." Certainly, this is a messenger (Greek αγγελος [*angelos*]) but Mark doesn't emphasize the showy or supernatural aspects of this person.

> For I handed on to you as of first importance what I in turn had received: that Christ died for our sins in accordance with the scriptures, and that he was buried, and that he was raised on the third day in accordance with the scriptures, and that he appeared to Cephas, then to the twelve.

The Gospel of Mark explains how we got here with this proclamation. Here's how it ends:

> Mary Magdalene, and Mary the mother of James, and Salome bought spices, so that they might go and anoint him.... They saw a young man who said to them, "Do not be alarmed; you are looking for Jesus of Nazareth, who was crucified. He has been raised; he is not here. Look, there is the place they laid him. But go, tell his disciples and Peter that he is going ahead of you to Galilee; there you will see him, just as he told you." So they went out and fled from the tomb, for terror and amazement had seized them; and they said nothing to anyone, for they were afraid. (Mark 16:1–8)

All we have here is an announcement from a mysterious young man, dressed in white. And it was so frightening they said nothing, not even conveying the message they'd been told to convey. This is, for many, a disturbing and unsatisfactory ending. Some ancient manuscripts had two different endings: one very briefly summarizing the ending of Matthew and a longer one, basically summarizing the end of Luke. Recognizing that these are not originally part of Mark, some scholars conjecture that the original manuscript of Mark was damaged and its ending was lost.[13]

Mark is comprehensible the way it is if we remember that its author did not set out to create a genre called "gospel"—rather he was setting out a compelling proclamation within the context of the church community that existed about three decades after the crucifixion and resurrection of Jesus. Ancient texts very often put the most important part at the center. The center of the Gospel of Mark is the account of the Transfiguration (9:28).[14]

---

13. While lots of manuscripts were damaged back then and incomplete texts survive, it strikes me as odd that the only copy that circulated was damaged at the end of a sentence and then it continued to circulate without emendation for a hundred years or more.

14. Being at the center of a text doesn't mean that the location is precisely calculated, just that the work flows toward the center and then resolves away from it. But I counted verses anyway, just to see if that held true here. From Mark 1:1 to Mark 16:8 there are 666 verses. (Yes, I know; I'm not a conspiracy theorist, but suit yourself.) The 333rd verse is Mark 9:10, "So they kept the matter to themselves questioning what this rising from the dead could mean." This is two verses after the Transfiguration proper, as the disciples are descending the mountain. Pretty close, considering that the verses were added later and

The Resurrection of Jesus

After Peter expressed the opinion that Jesus was the Messiah (8:29) and Jesus taught that he would "undergo great suffering, and be rejected by the elders, the chief priests, and the scribes, and be killed, and after three days rise again" (8:31), Jesus took Peter, James, and John up a high mountain where his clothes became dazzling white. Elijah and Moses were there in conversation with Jesus, and a voice from a cloud said, "This is my Son, the Beloved; listen to him!" (9:7).

I believe that this is the resurrection appearance of Jesus in the Gospel of Mark. The mysterious young man (likely an angel) says that the disciples will see Jesus in Galilee. This episode is placed in the Gospel near the end of Jesus' ministry in Galilee, shortly before he goes to Judea for the last phase of his ministry, which begins in chapter 10. The women are frightened and don't tell anyone, but the disciples are here in Galilee. In the remainder of chapter 9 are brief scenes that make more sense to me as issues in the post-resurrection church. In other words, this is not unlike the beginning verses of the book of Acts when he was "appearing to them during forty days and speaking about the kingdom of God" (1:3).

Mark was a text for the church to teach members who had already been converted, and probably baptized, the origin of the mystery of the one essential proclamation that unites them. Mark is short; it takes less than an hour and a half to read aloud to a gathering.[15] It can be absorbed as a single piece. The whole text is about the resurrection, and the resurrection is featured right in the center of the text. At the end, the disciples are left in fear, afraid to do as they are told—a realistic response of ordinary people to extraordinary events. But Jesus is right there in Galilee! His life in Galilee is defeating demons and the powers of death, healing, feeding, and forgiving. The gospel brings the church back to those things—the life that Jesus has brought, the resurrection that is for all in the real world: "The Son of Man is to be betrayed into human hands, and they will kill him, and three days after being killed, he will rise again" (Mark 9:31).

The resurrection is about life; in the Gospel of John, the term is "eternal life." But "eternal life" is not to be confused with "afterlife." Our current life is the life of the resurrection; when we are free from the powers that corrupt

---

aren't uniform in length!

15. Many thanks to Mother Ann Holt, who profoundly demonstrated this during Lent of 2018 when she gathered a group of us at Calvary Episcopal Church in Flemington, New Jersey; we took turns reading the entire Gospel of Mark aloud, beginning a bit after 10:00 a.m. and finishing in time to put together, serve the soup, and share our response to this experience while we ate at noon.

and destroy the creatures of God; when compassion toward those who are suffering or afraid is the most important thing about our life; when respect for the dignity of others is paramount; and when the prospect of losing or dying does not deter us from living generously. Real human beings do this all the time—it's not a matter of punctilious perfection in always being the most compassionate but in accepting the mercy and compassion of God and passing it along gratefully.

There is no way to see beyond the horizon of death. Our ideas and understandings of it are metaphors and speculations based on what is most important and valuable for us. And what is most important is life. Eternal life is continuous with this life we live now. The images in the Bible, which we take as depicting "heaven" or "immortality" or "afterlife," are metaphors that differ from one another. Paul discusses a body in the resurrection, but it has no context and is primarily just an assertion that life won't be attenuated but glorified. The book of Revelation piles on images, which are striking in their impact, but they can't be made to depict a concrete or consistent mode of life—they are metaphors for the triumph of the mercy, power, and life of God; the comfort of the witnesses; and the healing of all suffering. It would be wrong to attempt to reconcile the contradictory images of the Bible. To do so would reduce the promise of life to our impoverished imaginings; our choices would not only be less than the glory of God but would introduce limits and contentions that exclude possibilities that God does not exclude.[16] Long ago, I suffered a psychiatric episode which was either caused by or resulted in the collapse of all my ideas about the church, of any success in a career as a parish priest, and ultimately of my marriage and family. When I emerged from the consequent clinical depression, I stopped fearing death altogether. I realized that was just as much a delusion as my callow and self-serving fantasies about how wonderful the church would be with such a great leader as myself. Faith—that is to say, trusting God—is a

---

16. I think this applies even to the theological debate between those who assert universal salvation and those who assert that some are saved and others are not (thus the existence of hell and what categories of folk might be in it). In the New Testament, the most frequent mentions of hell and its equivalents are attributed to Jesus. Consistently, these are condemnations of those who hurt or demean the powerless—those allied or promoting the powers of death. In the context of our present reality, this has real meaning about the intent of God's love and the condemnation of demonic and death-dealing forces and people. Yet making those metaphors into eternal and static realities misses their point. The living God is compassion—fierceness against evil is a component of compassion; but over the horizon of physical death, we have no idea how that will work out. We know only that it is in line with the mercy that brings us eternal life.

matter of accepting God's limitless compassion and not needing to be the leading figure in the salvation of the world. I am confident that when I die, I will be enfolded in the love of the limitless life of the Source of our immense universe—whatever shape beyond shape that may take.

> You only are immortal, the creator and maker of mankind; and we are mortal, formed of the earth, and to the earth shall we return. For so did you ordain when you created me, saying, "You are dust, and to dust you shall return." All of us go down to the dust; yet even at the grave we make our song: Alleluia, alleluia, alleluia. (*1979 Book of Common Prayer*, 499)

9

The Spirit and the Church

In October 2014, when I was the theological librarian at the General Theological Seminary of the Episcopal Church, there was a meeting of our faculty union in my living room concerning an ongoing job action.[1] I received a phone call in the middle of the meeting. The senior warden of Trinity Episcopal Church of Morrisania in the south Bronx was seeking a priest to lead services and preach for the next few months—was I interested? I said I'd have to think about it. I called my wife, who told me I absolutely should do it; so before the afternoon was over, I called the warden and arranged to do services beginning on November 2—All Saints Sunday.

Allen Newman, Trinity's priest-in-charge, had just retired to Florida in September. Later, I learned that shortly after his retirement, Allen discovered that a very aggressive cancer had recurred. It progressed even faster than expected and he died November 1.

When I came to do the service on All Saints Sunday, both wardens of the parish were down in Florida to be with their priest as he was dying and to comfort his husband. The congregation at Trinity Episcopal Church of Morrisania was filled with grief and hurt that All Saints Sunday morning. And I learned from the announcements that one of their most important lay leaders was also in the hospital, near death from cancer.

---

1. Anyone seeking information about this situation can consult: Otterman, "Seeking Dean's Firing," the October 2014 archive of my blog (https://drewkadel.wordpress.com/2014/10/), or this website for the General Theological Seminary Faculty Union: http://www.safeseminary.net/.

The Spirit and the Church

For all of the month leading up to that All Saints Sunday, I had been filled with anger. At morning prayer and evensong, lines from the psalms, especially the imprecatory psalms, would light up my thoughts: "For there is no truth in their mouth, there is destruction in their heart" (Ps 5:9). "My lying foes who would destroy me are mighty. Must I then give back what I never stole?" (Ps 69:5). "How long, O God, will the adversary scoff? Will the enemy blaspheme your name forever?" (Ps 74:9). "See how they tremble with fear, because God is in the company of the righteous" (Ps 14:5). During our faculty action, there had been so many accusations and descriptions of our behavior that were utterly detached from reality that everything had started sounding like an attack, even the tone on my phone notifying me of a text message. This was not good for me spiritually; I was being eaten up from the inside.

At Trinity, I encountered an extraordinary community. Elaborate high church liturgy with incense at every opportunity, yet startlingly informal, with people darting in and out of the altar area frequently and unexpectedly. People mostly wore their Sunday best; many of the women wore hats, sometimes elaborate ones. What stood out to me most was the attentiveness and mutual respect of the members of the congregation. The congregation was almost entirely Black, mostly immigrants from the Caribbean or descendants of West Indian immigrants. The culture of Antigua, Jamaica, and the Virgin Islands permeated the service and the coffee hour (more accurately a luncheon) that followed the service. For All Saints Sunday, the youth choir sang. It was a large group, twenty-five or thirty children from age six through teenaged high schoolers, who were mostly brought to church by their grandparents.

They loved being together. They loved their church building, which was beautifully appointed in a conservative old-style fashion, with dark wood pews, the texts of the Ten Commandments stenciled above the stained-glass windows of the nave, and the Nicene Creed likewise under the clerestory windows—all in the language of the *1928 Book of Common Prayer*. Behind the ceramic-tiled altar were paintings of John the Baptist, St. Peter, and Jesus, whose physical characteristics resembled nineteenth and twentieth-century English and Germans rather than anyone who ever lived in Palestine or the Caribbean.

Morrisania was founded in the mid-nineteenth century as a village for middle-class commuters to New York City, which could be seen from the heights on Boston Road. By the 1930s, it had become an area where immigrants from the islands could afford to live, and in the 1950s, the New York City Housing Authority tore down much of the neighborhood around the church and built the Forest Houses projects. While most of the families at Trinity had lived within a few blocks of the church at one time, they had largely relocated to other parts of the city, especially during that period of time known as "the burning of the Bronx" that devastated the south Bronx in particular. Although the neighborhood was still very poor, and many of the parishioners had followed the path of other immigrant groups to the US into middle-class professional lives and the suburbs, they returned to their church to worship God in the beauty of holiness, to join in a community that had supported them their whole lives, and to enjoy their Caribbean cultures and food.

Their hospitality and generosity were manifest when I arrived. But so also was quite a bit of uncertainty and apprehension. The priest who had loved them and lived in their rectory for the past seven years had died; the lay leader who trained the acolytes, organized activities, did tireless work around the church building, and maintained connections with other south Bronx churches was in hospital, unlikely to recover; and their two elected leaders were a thousand miles away grieving their friend and pastor and supporting his husband in his grief. It was also beginning to sink in that the finances of the church were more precarious than they had realized. They looked to me. I had prepared a sermon on the Beatitudes for All Saints Sunday. It was about all of them as a model of Christian spirituality. When I heard that Father Allen had died, I expanded the "Blessed are those who mourn":

> We mourn and we hurt. The comfort that God gives does not take that hurt away, or explain away our sorrow. God comforts us by traveling the road with us, healing our hurts and giving mercy.

We prayed. The custom at Trinity was, at the end of the service, after communion and before the final blessing, the priest would offer individual blessings with anointing at the chancel step for whoever wanted to come forward. Blessings for travel, for birthdays or anniversaries, or for illness. The line on my first Sunday was quite long.

Toward the end of the blessings, I particularly remember one boy, about eight years old, who asked for prayers for his grandfather who'd recently had a heart attack. He was very serious and clearly worried. I asked his grandfather's name, Boswell Joseph Barrett. I prayed and anointed him. It was only much later, after I had gotten to know Joe Barrett well, that I learned that the only person who used the name Boswell was this grandson, who was also named Joseph. (Jo-Jo, as he was called, regarded himself and not his grandfather to have the exclusive rights to Joseph as his first name.) A retired attorney and police detective, Joe Barrett took great pleasure in being able to help others, especially organizing activities for neighborhood kids or giving legal advice to people who couldn't afford a lawyer. He told me that he met his wife because he was on sentry duty near the end of the Korean war and almost shot an "infiltrator," who turned out to be a starving kid rummaging through the camp's garbage. He decided to take the kid to a nearby orphanage, which is where he met Chang, who worked there. Ultimately, he served time in the brig for marrying a Korean national, which was against Army policy. Nearly seventy years later, he still glowed when he talked about her.

Trinity Church of Morrisania was filled with all sorts of people—accomplished and well-to-do and not so well-off, hard-working people. Some generous, some complainers, some wise, and some a bit silly. The silliest of all—and that was the general congregational opinion, not mine—was a woman who told me, after I had been there quite a while, that I was an "honorary Black person." My relationship with the congregation was based on being myself (a white American from the western deserts) and recognizing the people in the congregation as the individuals who they were, including their culture and experience of living in racialized America. The thing that particularly characterized this congregation was the high value they placed on dignity and respect—even respecting the dignity of someone who everyone agreed was a silly person, or even people who had offended someone or otherwise gotten out of line.

It was in being with this congregation weekly that my fierce anger subsided and I was healed. The institution where I was employed was overseen by some of the most prominent and powerful people in the church, and they resorted quickly to disrespecting the teachers of their students when they raised concerns about their management. This small church, which was under great stress and uncertainty about their future, consistently included me in the same respect they gave each other and their neighbors. And they needed and accepted my compassion and respect for them. Being able to extend care for people with real hurts and concerns enabled me to get outside my own hurt and anger.

Christian churches have been in decline for quite some time now. I started seminary in 1976 and was ordained in 1981. All through that time, people had been talking about that decline, and it has accelerated during my entire life as a priest. Mostly, the decline is talked about in terms of numbers—attendance numbers, numbers of baptisms, weddings, ordinations, numbers of parishes, and clergy employed by parishes. But the decline that I see is mostly in whether anyone trusts the church and whether the church gives people anything worth trusting.

I attend church conventions and listen to the pastors of the wealthiest churches argue against any program that would give more money to congregations with few resources, or projects to support immigrants or the homeless, by insisting that they have nothing to spare. And besides, their programs are the most successful and important ministries in the diocese. When times get tight financially, the first things cut are staff for spiritual care or work with the poor—building projects and the corpus of endowments are protected from cuts as long as possible. I've sometimes even heard it said by smart people that the Episcopal Church should be happy to concentrate its resources in a few big churches in urban areas and encourage the rest to pack up and close. Like most contemporary nonprofits, this results in great deference to the rich and powerful who may be big donors—though in my experience, many take advantage of this deference without opening their wallets in any significant way.

But it's not just that they don't pay any attention to the Epistle of James:

> My brothers and sisters, do you with your acts of favoritism really believe in our glorious Lord Jesus Christ? For if a person with gold rings and in fine clothes comes into your assembly, and if a poor person in dirty clothes also comes in, and if you take notice of the one wearing the fine clothes and say, "Have a seat here, please," while to the one who is poor you say, "Stand there," or, "Sit at my feet," have you not made distinctions among yourselves, and become judges with evil thoughts? Listen, my beloved brothers and sisters. Has not God chosen the poor in the world to be rich in faith and to be heirs of the kingdom that he has promised to those who love him? But you have dishonored the poor. Is it not the rich who oppress you? Is it not they who drag you into court? Is it not they who blaspheme the excellent name that was invoked over you? (James 2:1–6)

The decline of the church comes from cleaving to these ways of the world that honor power and dismiss compassion as if it is a frill, rather than the real work of the church. Is it any surprise that abuse is widespread in every denomination? That sexual abuse of women and children is now something

The Spirit and the Church

that people expect to emerge from churches? And apart from sexual abuse, there are all manner of ways that our authorities become authoritarian, demeaning people who question their priorities and exploiting vulnerable people, especially those who are fragile and in need of comfort and attention.

So, we wonder why people have started to choose to avoid our churches.

Were we to follow Jesus, church would be a place of compassion and healing. It is certainly true and possible. That is what I found at Trinity Episcopal Church of Morrisania in the south Bronx. Christian community is always messy, and as Dietrich Bonhoeffer reminds us, it is a dangerous delusion to think a community could be or should be ideal.[2] Everyone who enters a church is in need of compassion and mercy—that mercy is often needed because of misdeeds and dysfunction, as well as hurts or being marginalized. But compassion and mercy should not be confused with indulging abuse and hurting others, especially when leaders harm vulnerable people. Jesus had something to say about that:

> If any of you put a stumbling-block before one of these little ones who believe in me, it would be better for you if a great millstone were fastened around your neck and you were drowned in the depth of the sea. (Matt 18:6)

Compassion is care for the good of the other person; it's the way to healing of the spirit. Usually, we think of that as tenderness and comfort, and it very much is that way most of the time. But Jesus, who is all compassion, sometimes shows the other side of that—the fierceness at those who cause suffering. It is compassion and healing not only for those who have been made to suffer, but also to those who have been seduced by their own status and power and have forgotten who it is that they serve.

The inclination of those high in organizations to cover up these problems when they are done by friends or longtime associates or bosses saps the vitality and integrity of the church. It is yet another way that our institutions have come to serve mammon rather than God.

In the twentieth chapter of the Gospel of John, Jesus appears to his disciples who had hidden themselves away and locked the door. They were terrified about all that had happened: the crucifixion of Jesus, the anger of the crowds, and the Roman army's harshness in the face of the perceived threat of civil disorder. The whole town, their whole world, was filled with terror.

---

2. Bonhoeffer, *Life Together*, 26–30; originally written for his students at Finkenwalde, an underground seminary, and published in 1939 as *Gemeinsames Leben*.

Jesus appears out of nowhere and says, "Peace be with you." As it sinks in that he's really there, he says it again, "Peace, be with you. As the father has sent me, so I send you." Then he breathes on them, "Receive the Holy Spirit. If you forgive the sins of anyone, they are forgiven them; if you hold anyone fast, they are held fast" (John 21:19–23).[3] The Holy Spirit is God's love, God's compassion. Its presence is what defines and comprises the church. The fearful disciples are healed by Jesus' presence and given that love—and it's clear that it was given precisely so that they could help others and hold them close in a world that wants to reject and destroy them. The Holy Spirit is not about power as we typically understand that word. There's nothing coercive in God's compassion; there is no human office or authority that controls the use of that Spirit. There is no place to be proud in receiving or giving God's Spirit—it's a matter of holding one another when we need to be held.

In a church with a heritage of Trinitarian language arising out of the controversies of the fourth century, those of us who are theologically inclined tend to want more when we talk about the Holy Spirit—"a *person* of the Trinity! What's her resume? How do we describe him? The Spirit must be something else besides love!" To this I say, "What else is there besides Love?"

> God is love, and those who abide in love abide in God, and God abides in them. (1 John 4:16)

When God is known, what we know is love. I have been using the word compassion most of the time in this book. Love is a most excellent word, but many meanings have accreted to the word love. Often people regard love as a feeling—often one of desire or of having all one's desires met. But "compassion" is far less about feeling and far more an orientation toward the good of others—more specifically, to the person who needs compassion, mercy, and healing. St. Paul's well-known "hymn to love" in 1 Cor 13 is about the Holy Spirit. Paul has been discussing spiritual gifts for the entire previous chapter ("There are varieties of gifts, but the same Spirit" (1 Cor 12:4)). Paul concludes his description of the working of the Holy Spirit in terms of this kind of love.[4]

---

3. Sandra Schneiders, IHM, gave a lecture correcting this mistranslation in her course on the "Spirituality of the Gospel of John" at the Jesuit School of Theology at Berkeley in 1981. I give a more detailed summary of what she said in a footnote on this passage in the previous chapter.

4. Paul uses the Greek word αγαπη (agape). There is a whole literature on the

The Spirit and the Church

> And if I have prophetic powers, and understand all mysteries and all knowledge, and if I have all faith, so as to remove mountains, but do not have love, I am nothing. If I give away all my possessions, and if I hand over my body so that I may boast, but do not have love, I gain nothing.
> Love is patient; love is kind; love is not envious or boastful or arrogant or rude. It does not insist on its own way; it is not irritable or resentful; it does not rejoice in wrongdoing, but rejoices in the truth. It bears all things, believes all things, hopes all things, endures all things.
> Love never ends. But as for prophecies, they will come to an end; as for tongues, they will cease; as for knowledge, it will come to an end. For we know only in part, and we prophesy only in part; but when the complete comes, the partial will come to an end.
> (1 Cor 13:2–8)

Is it possible that the Holy Spirit is more than simply God's compassion lived out in this world? Certainly, it's possible that there is far more to God and God's actions than we can ever imagine or understand! But the Holy Spirit cannot be less or different than that. The Holy Spirit does not empower God's church or any people to be cruel, officious, or sanctimonious. Much is made in church circles, especially in the Episcopal Church, of the idea of "discernment." Too often, it's approached either as subjective choice ("how do I feel about this?") or as a management tool ("how will this fit with the goals of the organization?"). To the extent that the Spirit can be discerned, it is a matter of discerning compassion—and doing so for the present time in our concrete reality, not in the abstract for all eternity. What is compassion calling us to do (or to be) now, in this situation? It is thus that we are faithful, if faith has any meaning at all. People who have come to distrust church do so because there is so much evidence that compassion isn't the highest priority of organized religion; indeed, some people's experience is that compassion isn't even involved in the true motivation of the organizations they've encountered.

I have encountered both churches where compassion is consistently at the forefront, shaping their choices and life together, and organizations

---

Christian use of this word, distinguishing it from other Greek words that mean love. Much of the popular attention to it is overwrought, as if αγαπη is some extraordinary technical word, which it isn't. It just means love in the sense of like, care for, etc. I use "compassion" to avoid entering into linguistic arguments that are beyond my expertise, but also because it includes the sense of "mercy" and focuses on the one loved, instead of the person feeling or doing the loving.

where Christian language is used as a point of departure to rationalize control, self-serving pursuit of power, sanctimoniousness, and even cruelty. Often these things are mixed together to some extent. I do not know the future. Particularly, I don't know whether the denominations and organizations that have defined Christianity during my lifetime will thrive or survive in the long-term. I do know this, however: if the thing that defines our life together is anything other than the compassion of God and living that compassion, success will be worth nothing. Additionally, having had quite a bit of administrative experience and having lived with a spouse whose career has been reporting on businesses and finance, I'm convinced that approaches that seek to "run the church like a business" or "run the school like a business" are the least competent, businesslike, or successful at succeeding in sustaining themselves. It is not possible to permanently ensure the success of the church. There is no glory to be had in emulating the days when the prosperous church embodied the most privileged portions of society. There's no success to be gained by the service of mammon.

In John 14, Jesus says he will ask the Father, who will send another παρακλητος (*parakletos*)—rendered Paraclete in many translations. A literal rendering would be "one who is called to be with or alongside"—it's closely related to words meaning encouragement, comfort, and invite. It's often translated as "advocate," like a lawyer or person who aids another in getting their needs met—perhaps a comforter in times of grief, such as a priest. It is this word that Jesus uses to describe the Holy Spirit who he promises will be with his disciples. God standing alongside those who are discouraged, suffering, lost, or fearful, the Spirit is the compassion of God continuing among people, being alongside those who might be lost or in need of comfort. Thus, the Paraclete is not a fixed form but a shifting mutuality of encouragement. People rejoice in the presence of the Holy Spirit—some are tempted to confuse a joyful feeling with the Spirit, but compassion is not about feeling good—it's standing alongside others, giving encouragement, tenderness, and correction for their sake and for the sake of healing. It was in encouraging the people of Trinity Episcopal Church of Morrisania that I received healing—not in the least because they already partook of that Holy Spirit, the spirit of encouragement which they shared with me.

It is in the encouragement of that Holy Spirit that I have hope. Whether it is hope for the church as we think of it or of other manifestations of God's love among people, I don't know. We live because we have received mercy, and it's that mercy that we can give away.

10

The Deep

In the beginning when God created the heavens and the earth, the earth was a formless void and darkness covered the face of the deep, while a wind from God swept over the face of the waters.

—Genesis 1:12

So BEGINS THE BIBLE. "In the beginning" is the start of the story of God and God's people in time. It can also be as easily understood as "the origin"—the structure of how things are. Or both. The image of the deep is of water, uninterrupted, going on forever in all directions. In antiquity, this image would make sense. The sea was both familiar and dark, mysterious and dangerous—as were floods in the endless desert landscape where many of the authors of the Bible lived.[1] The first verses of the Bible portray chaos as vividly as we might describe the moments before the Big Bang, where there was only emptiness and no light.

"And God said, 'Let there be light'; and there was light" (Gen 1:3). With the coming of the light, the deep's formlessness took on form and illumination. This is the creation proper—God making something of significance out of a vastness that was truly nothing. Matter just drifting around in the void,

---

1. The flood in the Noah cycle is described as thus, "On that day all the fountains of the great deep burst forth, and the windows of the heavens were opened" (Gen 7:11). God was reversing God's work of creation, the thin shell we call the substantial earth and the dome we call the sky were dissolved, leaving Noah and his boat.

interacting or not at random, would have no meaning or significance without organization and direction. This is true whether or not one believes that God is a good way to talk about the origin of the universe. What I have come to believe is that this means the universe truly exists because of life, and, ultimately, life is founded in compassion—which is to say, I believe in God.

Though the deep—or the vastness of space-time, or what we might deem the ubiquity of entropy in every action and everything—is apparent to everyone, hardly anyone lives as if chaos is the ultimate reality. Clearly, some very intelligent people believe that chaos is the ultimate reality; but when I see what they really have to say (for instance, in absurdist theater), what I see is commentary on the struggles of living, the oppression of some by others, and the delusion of people who think that their self-absorbed way of living and thinking will rescue them from the realities of life. In other words, the presentation of absurdity is an assertion of life, usually decrying a world where people avoid compassion and fill their existence with emptiness. As far as I'm concerned, this is the furthest thing from living life as if all there is . . . is chaos. Those who really come close to living as if the ultimate reality is chaos are some who are severely mentally ill, to the point that nothing makes sense, and living or dying make no difference. Some sensitive people who are extremely depressed do take seriously that all may be chaos—but the only way out of the blackness of the worst of that sort of depression is to find a credible basis to somehow believe in life and living.

Instead, what I see is a world filled with life—all manner of living things, all sorts of possibilities, and the challenge to humans is to have the best possible life. Since light was spoken into existence, the deep has teemed with life. For those of us who live on the surface, the oceans, especially the deep parts, are a mysterious and alien world populated by creatures very different from ourselves and the animals we share the surface with.

I'm fascinated by whales, though I'm no expert of any sort. They're mammals like us, unlike their fellow dwellers of the deep like octopi, squids, and cuttlefish. They have complex social structures and communicate by making and interpreting sound. They have huge brains, much of which are dedicated to interpreting sounds—especially the echoes of their own sounds, which, in the darkness of the deep, allow them to make out distant shapes and other creatures—much as we use light to see mountains, buildings, and our friends approaching our house, looking forward to enjoying their company. Though there is no way to really know most of the life of these creatures of the deep, they have been observed expressing grief, love, and caring. The same is true, of course, of many other mammals, such as elephants or dogs. Having lived at close quarters with dogs for a couple of decades, it's clear to me that these animals have emotions like anxiety or enthusiasm—and care for specific people and other animals. I once read a blog post by a woman explaining the background of her line of championship bulldogs. The famous stud dog of her kennel had been the single puppy of the first litter of its mother. Because the knock on bulldogs was that they weren't good mothers and might smother the puppy, the puppy was kept in an incubator in the middle of a room. Momma dog didn't agree, however. When no one was around, she pushed the incubator over next to the desk. Then she pushed a chair next to the desk, hopped onto the chair, then the desk, and when the owner returned, she discovered the mother nursing the puppy in the incubator. So much for not being a good mother.[2] There are similar examples of complex problem-solving and animals that are motivated to go to great lengths to care for others.

The animals of the deep adapt and solve problems all the time, but since we aren't aquatic creatures by nature, it's hard to witness it. Recently, a pod of orcas off the coast of Spain were observed crashing into boats, taking rudders off sailboats, sometimes even sinking a craft or two. Apparently, they decided to do it as a sort of game, like the roughhousing kids or what we pay professional athletes to do on Sunday afternoons in the fall. The orca attacks might distress the boat owners, but it's hardly as distressing as the treatment various species of whales have received from humans over the past few hundred years.[3]

The complexity of behavior of the creatures of the deep is very different from the complexity of human behavior. Constructing "images" of the shape of the sea bed and the location of friends and food from echoing sounds is incomprehensible to me, yet it's everyday life for whales. They have no limbs and seldom use any sort of tools, which is humans' most distinctive characteristic—though it's clear from performances in captive environments like SeaWorld that it's not difficult for them to learn to manipulate objects when there's a reason to do so. People of all types, from philosophers, to laborers, to science fiction writers, have claimed that this characteristic makes humans superior to all creatures. But in the case of

---

2. The owner who wrote the piece was Darlene Stuedemann of Iowa. Her website is no longer available, but the name of her kennel was House of Beauty Bulldogs.

3. It goes without saying, perhaps, but Herman Melville's *Moby Dick* is both illustrative of this point and also of many aspects of human nature.

whales, at least, it's clear that "superior" merely means "like us"—like us in making systems of domination and exploitation; like us in making tools to make our lives easier, even if it involves enslavement of people or rendering the flesh of every alien intelligence we encounter into lamp oil or ivory for ornaments.

Human superiority is entirely about finding relatively short-term solutions for the convenience of those humans who have the most power—though short-term may mean for a lifetime or the duration of an empire. Progress, especially material progress, usually involves identifying a problem, big or small—something that is inconvenient, or unfair, or slow, or too expensive for the benefit received—and making something more convenient, fairer, quicker or cheaper. While there are plenty of exceptions, most of these changes that catch on really are better than what preceded them. The thing is, solutions are almost always envisioned as an improvement in the current context and people's imaginations don't really extend to social or environmental effects that will occur when that solution is adopted universally. In the late nineteenth and early twentieth century, automobiles were a way to get places faster, perhaps not having to bother with the troubles of maintaining a stable of horses. The advantages of driving in the open air through the limitless countryside made it almost inconceivable that air pollution caused by those cars would be among society's most serious problems by the end of the century, or that the patterns of accommodating to driving would reshape our built environment, making it impossible, for instance, to walk to the store in many whole regions. Johannes Gutenberg decided to print a Bible because wealthy customers, both institutional and individual, were willing to pay a lot for a nice, legible, formally written book.[4] The

---

4. There's a whole field of study on the production of medieval books called codicology. Basically, a manuscript Bible was a project for a team of skilled craftsmen working for over a year to produce a single copy. Estimating cost is very difficult, but during this century, St. John's University in Minnesota commissioned a project for an exquisite handwritten Bible. The initial estimate for the project was $3 million, but it ended up costing $8 million. Three hundred high quality reproductions were made, costing about $165,000 each. (See "Saint John's Bible" for more.) The St. John's Bible project isn't strictly comparable to fifteenth-century manuscript book production, but value equivalent to $100,000 for a fine, complete, large format Bible wouldn't be surprising. Gutenberg made 180 such books with his printing press with an effort not much greater than producing one or two equivalent copies in a scriptorium.

whole idea of the printing revolution that changed the face of European culture during the next century was not something he ever thought about.[5]

Perhaps the military contractors and university academics that put together the internet in the 1980s and 1990s thought about it becoming a universal communications system, but what people described as the reality and future of the internet in the 1990s was radically different than what has developed twenty-five to thirty years later.[6] People envisioned that the internet would build an entirely egalitarian society, free from the influence of big corporations. Instead, we got Marc Andreessen, Peter Theil, Jeff Bezos, Mark Zuckerberg, and Elon Musk. Problems were solved, the internet was refined and made easier for ordinary people to use, and new frontiers in the service of mammon were opened up. The results are, as always, ambiguous. Some things are better, some things are worse. Society and the values that people share have changed, but even those groups that have had measurable improvements, such as Black Americans or LGBTQ people, experience our present environment as particularly toxic and disempowering.

Our focus on tools increases the arrogance of *homo technicus*, the tool-makers. Big Tech, as it's sometimes called, harvests shocking fortunes by treating humans as objects—as aggregates that generate money and that can otherwise be dismissed. It's easy to become enamored of our tools and to regard them as more magical than they are. This delusion renders many, including the gentlemen mentioned above, into tools themselves. The speed with which computers can replicate calculations and all sorts of related tasks makes it seem like they are better than humans, rather than simply repeating tasks which humans have designed in a quick and efficient manner. We cannot get to a better world solely by making these machines better and faster. Without human compassion, that could not be a better world for humanity.

I use tools as much as anybody else because I'm entirely human. I wear clothes, I (usually) eat off plates (usually) with utensils—or at least when my wife is around. I'm writing on a computer. I spent a career as a librarian, organizing information resources to enable students and scholars to study better. I supervised the transition from card catalogs to online database access. In the later years, we discarded many books from overcrowded spaces

---

5. Elizabeth Eisenstein discusses the complex dynamics and intense cultural change following the invention of the printing press in her book *The Printing Press as an Agent of Change*. Many authors have continued this discussion.

6. Dave Karpf has great insight on this in his article, "25 Years of Wired Prediction." See also his forthcoming book on the topic.

and replaced them with electronic books and periodicals. I'm as much *homo technicus* as anyone else. Tool use is characteristic of our species, but tools are not the solution to happiness and human flourishing. Thoughtfulness, mutual support, and working with others and compassion are much bigger factors in successful societies. We are different from whales and other species, but I seriously doubt that we are superior in any way that's more meaningful than our self-assertion that we are.[7]

The title of this book is a question: how do you baptize a whale? Unlike a zen koan, it does have an answer—you can't baptize a whale. The fact that they are already immersed in water is only a small part of the problem. Here is a prayer from the baptismal service that describes the nature and purpose of baptism:

> We thank you, Almighty God, for the gift of water.
> Over it the Holy Spirit moved in the beginning of creation.
> Through it you led the children of Israel out of their bondage in Egypt into the land of promise. In it your Son Jesus received the baptism of John and was anointed by the Holy Spirit as the Messiah, the Christ, to lead us, through his death and resurrection, from the bondage of sin into everlasting life. We thank you, Father, for the water of Baptism. In it we are buried with Christ in his death. By it we share in his resurrection. Through it we are reborn by the Holy Spirit. Therefore in joyful obedience to your Son, we bring into his fellowship those who come to him in faith, baptizing them in the Name of the Father, and of the Son, and of the Holy Spirit.[8]

The first image is of the Holy Spirit moving over the *surface* of the water, and the next is the very human experience of going to the *land* of promise. Baptism is being buried with Christ in his death (an image derived from Paul in Rom 6:3–4). The death of Jesus is very specific—he was crucified by the Romans on a cross. That cross has been the chief symbol of Christianity throughout its existence. As simple in appearance as a cross might be, it is a very intentional and sophisticated tool. The victim is fixed to the crossbar by tying or nailing and suspended from it. The feet were usually secured to prevent kicking and moving around, but they were given no foothold. The force of gravity would eventually cause the victim's chest to collapse down on their lungs resulting in death by suffocation.

---

7. Maybe this sermon preached at Calvary Episcopal Church, Flemington, New Jersey, on October 8, 2017, that treats idolatry is relevant here: Kadel, "You Shall Not Bow."

8. *1979 Book of Common Prayer*, 306–7.

The Romans would have thought the guillotine totally inappropriate, since it was too efficient to accomplish the death by public torture—the entire point of crucifixion. For whales, all of this would be entirely meaningless. They live the bulk of their life under water—it's the source of sustenance for them, not death. Not only do they not make tools in their regular habitat, but a cross wouldn't achieve anything like its purpose underwater—bodies, whether cetacean or human, are too buoyant for gravity to succeed in its torture. Whales have their own joys and their own problems, I'm sure, but human stories, symbols, concepts, or sacraments are of no use to them. The ways in which the love of God is worked out among them is entirely their own and just as incomprehensible to us as ours are to them.

This whole book is about compassion. Compassion is not unique to humans, and, for the most part, we aren't even very good at it. However, I believe that, quite literally, compassion is the foundation of the universe. Absent caring, absent life, the void would still be a void with no significance whatsoever. This is why so much of this book is about Jesus. As Charles Wesley put it, "Jesus thou art all compassion, pure, unbounded love thou art."[9] The orthodox Christian teaching is that the universe was created through Christ, based in part on this passage in the letter to the Colossians:

> He is the image of the invisible God, the firstborn of all creation; for in him all things in heaven and on earth were created, things visible and invisible, whether thrones or dominions or rulers or powers—all things have been created through him and for him. (Col 1:15–16)

When coupled with the assertion that salvation is only through Jesus, this comes across as a narrow and parochial expression of Christian supremacism. As it's usually encountered, it also seems to have little to do with the Jesus we encounter in the New Testament, especially in the four canonical Gospels. But if we forswear our tendency to make abstractions and then develop rules from those abstractions, and instead regard Jesus concretely in the way he lived, healed, and confronted sanctimoniousness and oppression, a very different understanding of this passage emerges. The Jesus that is presented in the Gospels is the complete image of compassion—not some reduced essence but how compassion works in this world: deeply healing, merciful to ordinary people in the difficulties of their lives,

---

9. In the first verse of his hymn "Love divine, all loves excelling" found in the Episcopal Church's *Hymnal 1982* as hymn 657, as well as in countless other hymnals.

and courageous in protecting those who are oppressed and hurt by the strong and powerful.

That image cannot be complete without Jesus' crucifixion—no understanding of compassion is complete without the real stakes of facing evil in this world. The image is also not complete without Jesus' resurrection—death and cynicism are not the final word; the Compassion of God is the reality at the beginning and at the end. I have no expectation that whales or space aliens would find the story or image of Jesus meaningful,[10] though I fully expect that they understand and cherish compassion at a very deep level. Jesus is not the property of any church or collection of churches or the cultures they promote. Rather, the reality of the living image of perfect compassion places all our complacency and self-righteousness under judgment.

I use the word compassion in preference to other good words that also mean "love." One reason that I like to use compassion is that it pretty clearly includes mercy as an essential facet. Anyone who has caused harm to others, acted selfishly, or willingly benefited from the suffering of others[11] would be forever alienated from the community of the compassionate if they didn't receive mercy. Some people believe that they have not done those things and that mercy isn't that important. I regard such people as examples of self-righteousness, another act for which they can, perhaps, receive mercy from others who recognize it as a problem. To the extent that church has any greater meaning beyond its members and buildings, it is as a community of those who receive mercy.

Compassion includes humility. Those of us who are often arrogant find that being that way makes it difficult, impossible really, to make the well-being of someone else the true first priority. Things may get done, some of them beneficial, but it's our accomplishment and self-regard that's the priority. No wonder that we are so far from healing the curse of racism among white Americans—and I include liberals and progressives in that category. Humans have failed to have the requisite humility throughout history, at least throughout the history of Europe and its continuation on the American continent. We title our species *sapiens*—wise. Wisdom requires humility about what we know and what we don't. But that's commonly

---

10. If they somehow came to the point of decoding it, they might glean from it some understanding of the bloody-mindedness and cruelty that characterize so much of the human behavior they might observe.

11. Not to put too fine a point on this, but this includes the person writing this and the person reading it.

ignored in the rush to subdue and control everything. We *are* created in the image of God, but that image is not being smarter or more dominant; the image of God is the Compassionate One—the one that the arrogant, dominant, and sanctimonious ones decided to put on a cross. We are created in the image of the compassionate source of our universe, we just need to live like it sometimes.

Pope Francis said, "I would baptize a Martian if he wanted me to." But who is he, as a human being, to say what an alien intelligence, space alien or whale, could benefit from a human sacrament given for humans? They live fully in God's compassionate universe—the forms of God's compassion for them are as incomprehensible to us as crucifixion is to a creature whose entire life is lived submerged in the depths of the ocean. It is humans who need to be baptized. Baptized in God's mercy and in forgiveness. Forgiveness even for those who would put God's people on the cross of racism, greed, and arrogance.

There is nothing more important than compassion and living compassionately. It's the most ordinary state of people, from the time they are born, yet it's also a lifelong project that requires great effort. We are often disappointed—often because of actions of others, but also because we ourselves are unwilling and lack the courage to make the sacrifices involved in caring for one another at difficult times. It is often fragmentary in our experience of it, but compassion is real. Compassion is possible. Life is possible. The thing is to live it fully.

Te Deum Laudamus

When I was a child, the main Sunday service at St. David's Episcopal Church in Caldwell, Idaho, alternated between Holy Communion and Morning Prayer. It was a small church with a tiny volunteer choir. In Morning Prayer, the entire congregation would join in singing the canticles. At five years old, this was the main part that I liked in the service. Regularly, we would sing the *Te Deum Laudamus* and it became a foundation of my spirituality. While performances of the *Te Deum* were often historically big affairs for major events in church and state, with many grand musical settings of the text, I prefer the simple tune we sang: numbers 613 and 617 in the *Hymnal 1940* by E. G. Monk and W. Croft. Even during years that I never thought of it, this text guided my understanding of God and God's people. I often sing it to myself in times of need, or reflection, or just times of joy.

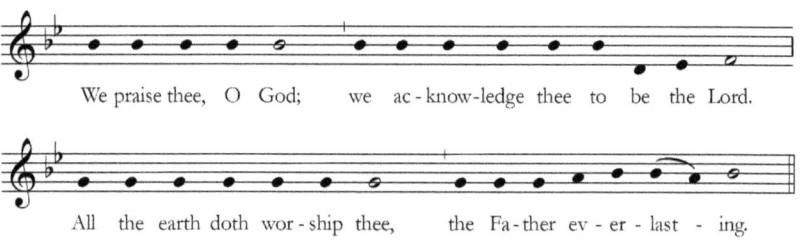

We praise thee, O God; we acknowledge thee to be the Lord.
All the earth doth worship thee, the Father everlasting.
To thee all Angels cry aloud; the Heavens, and all the Powers therein:
To the Cherubim and Seraphim continually do cry,
Holy, Holy, Holy, Lord God of Sabaoth;
Heaven and earth are full of the Majesty of thy glory.
The glorious company of the Apostles praise thee.
The goodly fellowship of the Prophets praise thee.

Te Deum Laudamus

The noble army of Martyrs praise thee.
The holy Church throughout all the world doth acknowledge thee;
The Father, of an infinite Majesty;
Thine adorable, true, and only Son;
Also the Holy Ghost, the Comforter.

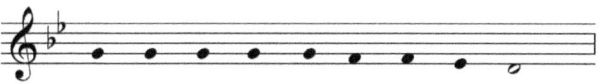
Thou art the King of glo-ry O Christ.

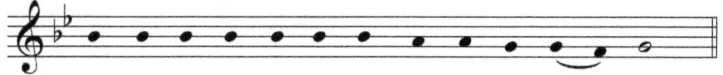
Thou art the ev-er-last-ing Son of the Fa-ther.

Thou art the King of Glory, O Christ.
Thou art the everlasting Son of the Father.
When thou tookest upon thee to deliver man,
    thou didst humble thyself to be born of a Virgin.
When thou had overcome the sharpness of death,
    thou didst open the Kingdom of Heaven to all believers.
Thou sittest at the right hand of God, in the glory of the Father.
We believe that thou shalt come to be our Judge.

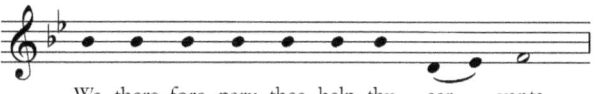
We there-fore pary thee help thy ser-vants,

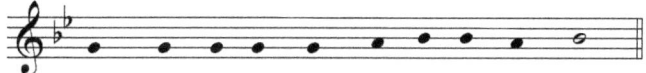
whom thou hast re-deemed with thy pre-cious blood.

We therefore pray thee, help thy servants,
    whom thou hast redeemed with thy precious blood.
Make them to be numbered with thy Saints, in glory everlasting.
O Lord, save thy people, and bless thine heritage.
Govern them, and lift them up for ever.
Day by day we magnify thee;
And we worship thy Name ever, world without end.
O Lord, have mercy upon us, have mercy upon us.

How Do You Baptize a Whale?

O Lord, let thy mercy be upon us, as our trust is in thee.
O Lord, in thee have I trusted; let me never be confounded.
(*Book of Common Prayer 1928*, 10–11)

For Further Reading

Barth, Karl. *Church Dogmatics*. Edinburgh, UK: T. & T. Clark, 1955.
———. *The Epistle to the Romans*. Oxford: Oxford University Press, 1933.

> Karl Barth is regarded by many as the twentieth century's most important Christian theologian. At the end of World War I, he published *The Epistle to the Romans*, which strikingly rejected the naturalistic, philosophical interpretation of Christianity of nineteenth century theologians and asserted the transforming power of the Word of God (Jesus Christ). He was neither fundamentalist nor conservative in this protest and his writing can be quite striking. However, reading his works is challenging, even for professional theologians—each of the *Church Dogmatics* twelve "part volumes" is about eight hundred pages, with large sections in small print.

Beard, Mary. *SPQR: A History of Ancient Rome*. New York: Norton, 2015.

> A professor of Classics at Cambridge University, Beard presents an accessible one-volume history of Rome and its conquests. The three centuries between 100 BCE and 200 CE occupy the largest portion of the book. These set the political context for the ministry of Jesus and the New Testament.

Bonhoeffer, Dietrich. *Letters and Papers from Prison*. Edited by Eberhard Bethge. New York: Simon & Schuster, 1971.
———. *Life Together*. New York: Harper & Row, 1954.

> Bonhoeffer was a German theologian who was imprisoned by the Nazis in 1943 and executed in April 1945. *Life Together* is based on lectures he gave to his students at an underground seminary in the late 1930s, and *Letters and Papers from Prison* are letters and documents mostly smuggled out during his time at an interrogation prison in Berlin. He's known for important theological insights, but I'm particularly impressed with his pastoral sensitivity, connecting

theology with encouragement for everyone he encountered during the horrors of World War II.

Gafney, Wilda. *Womanist Midrash: A Reintroduction to the Women of the Torah and the Throne.* Louisville, KY: Westminster John Knox, 2017.

> An African-American scholar of the Hebrew Bible examines passages from the first five books of the Bible, including the stories of women and their contributions as well as careful examinations of well-known passages where our assumptions about what they say about gender and related topics are questioned.

Graeber, David. *Debt: The First 5,000 Years.* Brooklyn: Melville House, 2011.

———, and David Wengrow. *The Dawn of Everything: A New History of Humanity.* New York: Farrar, Straus and Giroux, 2021.

> David Graeber was an anthropologist and activist whose ideas and advice brought about the Occupy Wall Street movement—he died in 2020, shortly before his book written with archaeologist David Wengrow was published. Graeber and Wengrow challenge the assumptions of philosophers, historians, and social scientists about the evolution of past and present structures of human societies—especially those things, like the nation state, that many assume are inevitable. They explore evidence from recent anthropological research that societies going as far back as thirty thousand years organized themselves in successful societies that differed widely from one another in structure and values, even when they existed close to one another in time and space.

Hart, David Bentley. *The New Testament: A Translation.* New Haven: Yale, 2017.

> This is an extraordinary translation of the New Testament by a single scholar. Refusing to homogenize the different styles and roughness of the various documents of the early Christian church, Hart reveals the strangeness and intensity of faith expressed in the letters of St. Paul, the distinct voices of the four evangelists in their Gospels, and the exuberant imagery and sometimes ungrammatical writing of the seer of the book of Revelation.

Homer. *The Iliad.* Translated by Emily Wilson. New York: Norton, 2023.

———. *The Odyssey.* Translated by Emily Wilson. New York: Norton, 2018.

> Emily Wilson's translations of the oldest written texts of the classics are a pleasure to read. Her rhythmic poetry brings home that these were originally oral poems that were meant to be sung aloud and listened to. I was struck by the prominence of religious

observance throughout these poems, in particular the emphasis on proper sacrifice.

Schneiders, Sandra. *The Revelatory Text: Interpreting the New Testament as Sacred Scripture*. 2nd ed. Collegeville, MN: Liturgical Press, 1999.
———. *Written That You May Believe: Encountering Jesus in the Fourth Gospel*. Revised and expanded ed. New York: Crossroad, 2003.

My references to Sandra Schneiders come from my memory and class notes from her class "The Spirituality of the Gospel of John" at the Jesuit School of Theology at Berkeley in the Spring of 1981. She was a marvelous and dynamic lecturer! The books listed above give a fuller and more recent account of her approach to Scripture and Jesus in the Gospel of John.

Stringfellow, William. *My People Is the Enemy: An Autobiographical Polemic*. Eugene, OR: Wipf & Stock, 2005. Originally published: Holt, Rinehart and Winston, 1964.
———. *An Ethic for Christians and Other Aliens in a Strange Land*. Eugene, OR: Wipf & Stock, 2004. Originally published: Word, 1973.
———. *Conscience and Obedience: The Politics of Romans 13 and Revelation 13 in Light of the Second Coming*. Eugene, OR: Wipf & Stock, 2004. Originally published: Word, 1977.
———. *The Politics of Spirituality*. Eugene, OR: Wipf & Stock, 2006. Originally published: Westminster, 1984.

Bill Stringfellow was a lawyer, activist, and lay theologian. He addressed the political and social landscape of America from the 1950s to the 1980s through his understanding of the Bible and autobiographical analysis. His use of the principalities and powers of the New Testament to understand the behavior of contemporary institutions and social forces has been very influential for later theology and Christian activists. Stringfellow is best understood as a voice seeking, with his readers, to be "Living Humanly in the Midst of Death," which is the title of one section of *An Ethic for Christians and Other Aliens in a Strange Land*. (His work is listed in historical order here.)

Bibliography

1979 Book of Common Prayer. New York: Church Publishing, 1979.
Adams, Douglas. *The Ultimate Hitchhiker's Guide to the Galaxy.* New York: Del Ray, 2002.
AFP. "The Pope Says Baptism for All — Even Martians." The Sydney Morning Herald, May 13, 2014. https://www.smh.com.au/world/pope-says-baptism-for-all--even-martians-20140513-zraqo.html.
Barth, Karl. *Church Dogmatics.* Edinburgh, UK: T. & T. Clark, 1955.
———. *The Epistle to the Romans.* Oxford: Oxford University, 1933.
Beard, Mary. *SPQR: A History of Ancient Rome.* New York: Norton, 2015.
Book of Common Prayer (1928): And Administration of the Sacraments and Other Rites and Ceremonies of the Church. New York: Church Pension Fund, 1945.
Bonhoeffer, Dietrich. *Letters and Papers from Prison.* Edited by Eberhard Bethge. New York: Simon & Schuster, 1971.
———. *Life Together.* New York: Harper & Row, 1954.
Carlowicz, Michael. "An Eagle Takes Off for Home." NASA Earth Observatory, July 20, 2019. https://earthobservatory.nasa.gov/images/145332/an-eagle-takes-off-for-home.
"Death of Dean Hoffman; Head of General Theological Seminary Expired on a Train." The New York Times Archives, June 18, 1902. https://www.nytimes.com/1902/06/18/archives/death-of-dean-hoffman-head-of-general-theological-seminary-expired.html.
Eisenstein, Elizabeth. *The Printing Press as an Agent of Change: Communications and Cultural Transformations in Early Modern Europe.* Cambridge: Cambridge University Press, 1979.
Gafney, Wilda. *Womanist Midrash: A Reintroduction to the Women of the Torah and the Throne.* Louisville, KY: Westminster John Knox, 2017.
Gaiman, Neil, and Terry Pratchett. *Good Omens: The Nice and Accurate Prophecies of Agnes Nutter, Witch.* New York: Workman, 1990.
Graeber, David. *Debt: The First 5,000 Years.* Brooklyn: Melville House, 2011.
Graeber, David, and David Wengrow. *The Dawn of Everything: A New History of Humanity.* New York: Farrar, Straus and Giroux, 2021.
Hart, David Bentley. *The New Testament: A Translation.* New Haven: Yale, 2017.
Homer. *The Iliad.* Translated by Emily Wilson. New York: Norton, 2023.
———. *The Odyssey.* Translated by Emily Wilson. New York: Norton, 2018.
The Hymnal 1982: According to the Use of the Episcopal Church. New York: Church Publishing, 1985.

Bibliography

Hymnal of the Protestant Episcopal Church 1940. New York: Church Hymnal Corporation, 1940.

Josephus, Flavius. *Flavius Josephus, Translation and Commentary*. Edited by Steve Mason. Leiden, NL: Brill, 2000.

Kadel, Drew. "You Shall Not Bow Down to Them or Worship Them." Observations, Oct. 8, 2017. https://drewkadel.wordpress.com/2017/10/07/you-shall-not-bow-down-to-them-or-worship-them-2/.

Karpf, David. "25 Years of Wired Predictions: Why the Future Never Arrives." Wired, September 18, 2018. https://www.wired.com/story/wired25-david-karpf-issues-tech-predictions/.

Lasseter, John, dir. *Toy Story*. Los Angelos: Pixar, 1995.

Marshall, Aarien. "Why the Global CrowdStrike Outage Hit Airports So Hard." Wired, July 19, 2024. https://www.wired.com/story/crowdstrike-windows-outage-airport-travel-delays/.

Otterman, Sharon. "Seeking Dean's Firing, Seminary Professors End Up Jobless." New York Times, Oct. 2, 2014. https://www.nytimes.com/2014/10/02/nyregion/labor-dispute-leaves-professors-jobless.html

"The Saint John's Bible, Heritage Edition: Introduction." Santa Clara University Library, Sept. 27, 2024. https://libguides.scu.edu/saintjohnsbible#.

Schneiders, Sandra. *The Revelatory Text: Interpreting the New Testament as Sacred Scripture*. 2nd ed. Collegeville, MN: Liturgical Press, 1999.

———. *Written That You May Believe: Encountering Jesus in the Fourth Gospel*. Revised and expanded ed. New York: Crossroad, 2003.

Shakespeare, William. *The Yale Shakespeare, The Complete Works*. Edited by Wilbur L. Cross and Tucker Brooke. New York: Barnes & Noble, 1993.

Smith, Christian, and Melissa Denton. *Soul Searching: The Religious and Spiritual Lives of American Teenagers*. New York: Oxford University, 2006.

Stringfellow, William. *Conscience and Obedience: The Politics of Romans 13 and Revelation 13 in Light of the Second Coming*. Eugene, OR: Wipf & Stock, 2004.

———. *An Ethic for Christians and Other Aliens in a Strange Land*. Eugene, OR: Wipf & Stock, 2004. Originally published: Word, 1973.

———. *My People Is the Enemy: An Autobiographical Polemic*. Eugene, OR: Wipf & Stock, 2005. Originally published: Holt, Rinehart and Winston, 1964.

———. *The Politics of Spirituality*. Eugene, OR: Wipf & Stock, 2006. Originally published: Westminster, 1984.

Unruh, John D. *The Plains Across: The Overland Emigrants and the Trans-Mississippi West, 1840–1860*. Urbana, IL: University of Illinois Press, 1979.

www.ingramcontent.com/pod-product-compliance
Lightning Source LLC
Chambersburg PA
CBHW070458090426
42735CB00012B/2606